Liberated Love

Passion 4 Purpose Publications

www.passion-4-purpose.com

SHICRETA MURRAY

Copyright © 2018 by Shicreta Murray

All rights reserved. Without prior written permission from the publisher, no part of this publication may be reproduced, stored in a retrievable system, or transmitted, in any form or by any means electronic, mechanical, photocopying, recording, or otherwise, except by the inclusion of brief quotations in review.

Unless otherwise indicated all scriptures are derived from the following Translations of the Holy Bible: Scripture taken from the New King James Version®. Copyright © 1982 by Thomas Nelson. Used by permission. All rights reserved.

The KJV King James Version is public domain.

Thayer's Greek-English Lexicon of the New Testament by Joseph H. Thayer, Copyright © 2017 by Hendrickson Publishers, Peabody, Massachusetts. Used by permission. All rights reserved.

Henry Matthew. Matthew Henry Whole Bible Commentary. Public Domain. 1706

Hope Alliance, Round Rock, TX 78664. Abuse Educational Material.

Public Education Information. Used by Permission.

Two Minds: The Cognitive Differences Between Men and Women, Spring 2017, Stanford Medicine Magazine. Article Written by Bruce Goldman.

https://stanmed.stanford.edu/2017spring/how-mens-and-womens-brains- are-different.html

www.vocabulary.com https://ncadv.org/statistics

https://www.cdc.gov/violenceprevention/pdf/ipv-nisvs-factsheet-v5-a.pdf

Library of Congress Control Number: 2018912672
ISBN-13: 978-0-9897960-9-5
Cover Design by
Shicreta Murray, Traverr, Amolbd, & Russell Smith
Back Cover Photo by
Edward William Jones edited by Russell Smith

Richmond, TX

Printed in the United States

DISCLAIMER

This book is not intended in any way to give the impression that every man is abusive or engages in abusive behaviors. Instead, this book is intended to create awareness of the quiet world of domestic abuse that exists within the Christian church. If the contents of this book offend you in any way, please know that offense is not the goal. However, if one chooses to embrace offense, one will miss the opportunity to help address the devastating and deadly issue of domestic abuse, which affects the Christian church just as much as it does society in general. Please read with the eyes of your mind and heart open. In addition, if any woman who has been affected by Christian teachings about relationships finds herself in an abusive relationship, she should seek outside counsel and guidance from her local domestic violence organizations. Please know that you are not alone, and that God will not be angry at you for seeking help.

DEDICATION

First, I dedicate this book to my mother, Donna. She has had trials similar to my own. Verbal and emotional domestic abuse has caused her to lose the gleam in her eyes. To my mother, I write...

Your example of spiritual strength taught me how to stand. Your weaknesses taught me how to live. All of your life choices taught me how to believe in God through Christ, to trust Him, to never give up, and to never allow myself to be overcome by any negative situation. Your sincere efforts to love taught me how to respond to God's love for me by loving myself and others. Thanks, Mom, for allowing God to use every facet of your life (the good, bad, and ugly) to teach me so much! I love you always, no matter what.

Second, I dedicate this book to every woman, both Christian and non-Christian, who is or has been the victim of domestic abuse. To you, I write...

To every woman who has been influenced by the teachings from the Christian church and who remained in an abusive domestic relationship even though it cost you your health, soul, and life; and to those who died trying to be faithful to what has been taught as God's order: Please know that your suffering or death has not been in vain. I believe that God desires to use this book to help vindicate every drop of your blood, restore your soul, and bring healing to your physical and emotional pain.

LETTER FROM THE AUTHOR

Having been raised as a woman within the Christian church all of my life, I have experienced and endured outright mistreatment and oppression from many men who held Bibles in their hands. My first experience occurred while I was being raised in a home where verbal and emotional abuse, disrespect, and the oppression of women were considered normal. Then, while growing up, I attended Christian services with my parents, and it became evident to me that within the public forum of the Christian church, women were always second to men. Finally, after waking up one day and finding myself the victim of domestic abuse at the hands of a man who was part of the Christian church and who also held a Bible in his hands, I'd had enough. I knew it was time for me to discover what was happening within the Christian church that was encouraging female oppression and domestic abuse, as well as creating such a huge gap between the male and female sexes. After spending enough time being beaten up by tyrannical men who held the same Bible that Christ uses to build me up, I figured it was time to confront the Christian teachings I had been raised to believe about men and women. So, I went on a journey to discover God's true heart toward men and women. In essence, this book embodies my personal voice in support of the "Me Too" and "Church Too" movements. It is evident that many women have had enough of the foolish behavior from many men both outside and inside the Christian church. For centuries, women have been raised to be regarded as less valuable and labeled as second to men. Therefore, many women have gone through literal hell at the hands of abusive and disrespectful men. I believe it is time for the Christian church to take responsibility for their role in condoning female oppression, excusing abusive behaviors toward women, and encouraging male dominance. For the record, this book does not intend to bash all men. Instead, it is designed to liberate women from oppression, break down the walls of division between females and males, and create a different perception of God's heart toward women and men. I hope you are as blessed by this book as I have been. Out of all the books out there, thanks for choosing mine to read. Be blessed!

Peace and Love in Christ,
Shicreta

For as he thinks in his heart, so is he.
"Eat and drink!" he says to you, But his heart is not with
you.
-Proverbs 23:7

"Jesus said to him, "If you can believe, all things are
possible to him who believes."
- Mark 9:23

"Belief is developed by how a person is taught to think.
A person's thoughts will develop and cultivate a person's
beliefs and create a person's overall perception of life.
Whatever a person believes a person will live out"
– Shicreta Murray

TABLE OF CONTENTS

INTRODUCTION

Considering that both Christian and non-Christian women—
and, hopefully, even some men—will be journeying with me
through this book, I will provide a quick lesson on the general perception of the Christian church for those who may
not have this information. Before I begin, let me clarify my
perception of the Christian church. When I say "Christian
church," I mean any denomination or non-denomination associated with Jesus Christ and the Bible i.e. Catholic, Method-
ist, Pentecostal, Lutheran, Baptist, non- denominational,
Church of Christ, etc. Yes, each denomination I mentioned
has a different biblical standard, but each one still claims to
believe in Jesus Christ and the Bible. Therefore, in my opinion, they all must be acknowledged as Christian.

First, let me say that the Christian Bible, which consists
of the Old and New Testaments, is the only book that Christians recognize as God's word. According to biblical standards, to be a Christian, one must gain his or her primary identity and fundamental beliefs from the New Testament commandments that God sent through His Son, Jesus Christ. So,
basically, the instructions that Jesus left are supposed to be
the only established foundation dictating the beliefs of an au-

thentic Christian. Most people perceive the Christian church as a group of people who gather weekly in a building and confess Jesus Christ as Savior. The standards for the marital relationship between a man and a woman come from the Bible. Once we realize how important the Bible is in establishing the foundation of the marital relationship, we will understand why so many people, Christians and non-Christians alike, seek a Christian minister to perform their wedding in a church building. One thing we must note is that, throughout history, the predominant leaders within the Christian church have been males. They have primarily been the ones who perceive and interpret what the Bible says and who convey those messages to members of the Christian church.

Now that you know what I mean when I say the "Christian church," hopefully, as a Christian woman, you'll understand why I am using this book to address the teachings and beliefs within the Christian church with pure love and concern. As a person who has attended the Christian church for many years, I am writing this book in a torn state of mind. On one hand, I feel like I am writing about my extended family, whom I know and love so dearly. On the other hand, I feel like I am writing about strangers whom I love but don't really know anymore. At some points, I feel like I am writing as an observer from the inside with detailed information, but yet, due to the pain I have experienced within the Christian church, I am also writing as one who stands outside, looking in from a different perception. As a Christian woman, I am questioning what I have seen and experienced throughout my years within the Christian church.

I am writing this book as one who has received just as many scars from many men within the Christian church as I have from many non-Christian men. However, as you will discover during our journey through this book, the perception of male and female relationships translated through the Christian church has created the standard for the foundation of relationships in most parts of the world. Sadly, I have observed how the perception of women maintained by most of the male- dominated leadership within the Christian church has caused tragedies in the lives of women throughout the world. Due to domestic abuse, many women have died or lost their souls and hearts for God. Some have even lost their sanity. Sadly, the perception of who is holding the Bible within the Christian church has made the beliefs within the Christian church responsible for the most hideous crimes committed throughout human history.

Eyes Wide Open

Several years ago, I had an encounter with God in which I heard the loud, thunderous, oceanic voice of Jesus speak to me and say, *"Go tell My people to get their hearts in order because I am coming soon."* Well, after that encounter, my life took dramatic turns, both positive and negative. The positive turn was that, since that encounter, God has given me the ability to outline His order and help people see life and relationships from His perspective. The negative turn was that, in one way or another, I usually have to experience what I write about. Unfortunately, I had to learn about the world of domestic abuse from a personal experience that ended my marriage. Being born a female and then raised as a Christian, I felt like I had two marks on my head. After my failed marriage, I felt very disappointed in the teachings within the Christian church. I felt as though some of the teachings within the Christian church misrepresented God's perception of men and women in a marital relationship. That misinformation opens the door to domestic abuse and leads many Christian women (like me) straight to divorce court. After that horrible experience, I promised myself that I would learn why most religious doctrines seem to oppress women, destroy men's minds, distort relationships, and cause domestic abuse. I also set out to learn about the roots of abuse and to teach both men and women how to overcome domestic abuse and reconnect with God and one another through a personal relationship with Jesus Christ.

Although, both males and females are victims of abuse, as you will learn in this book, it is a known fact that more women suffer from abuse at the hands of men than vice versa (see chapter 4 for statistics). This book will not only teach you Biblical perceptions about female oppression, including male and female relationships, it will also educate you about the dark, cold world of domestic abuse. We will expose and discuss the world of domestic abuse and detail two specific forms of abuse that I believe are used against women within the Christian church every day. These two off-center beliefs damage the overall relationship between men and women. We will also explore the misinterpretations of the Bible that are used to influence some Christian men to become abusers, as well as discover some of the reasons why many Christian women stay in abusive situations.

On my journey, through all my experiences, I have learned a lot about thought, belief, and perception. This book hinges mostly on how Christians think and create their beliefs, which in turn controls the way in which many men and women within the Christian church perceive and interpret the Bible, God, and one another. We will discuss the thoughts and beliefs of:

- How the Christian church teaches men and women to
- perceive one another,

- How God sees abuse and female oppression,

- How God actually perceives men and women,

- How God intends for men and women to think about and perceive Him,

- How God expects a husband and a wife to think about one another in marriage.

In essence, as a woman, this book is my voice of domestic violence awareness for the Christian church. I pray that you will enjoy your journey through the pages of this book. Fasten your seat belts as we learn the lessons and revelations I have discovered in my life – lessons and revelations that have taught me how to overcome abuse, discover true liberation as a woman, overcome the misrepresentations of God that the majority of the Christian church inadvertently enforces, and overcome the abusive and disrespectful behavior of many men—both Christian and non-Christian. Sadly, the essence of the foundational truths about God's original order for relationships seems to be the opposite of what most Christian churches teach. Consequently, it was the ups and downs of my life's journey that catapulted me into discovering what God's "Liberated Love" really looks like. Overall, I hope this book helps many of my Christian peers confront the bases of their teachings so that they can change their foundational beliefs and experience true liberated love. I hope

God can use this book to heal and liberate you just as He has used it to heal and liberate me! Be blessed and enjoy your journey!

CHAPTER 1

STANDARD FOR LIFE

Within the Christian church, the Bible is used as a standard for all relationships, from work relationships to marriage. The Bible establishes the foundation of what we require to have a healthy relationship with God. It also shows us what we require to have healthy relationships with others. For any relationship to flourish, a person must have a healthy perception of God as well as a healthy perception of the person whom they are in a relationship with. To have a healthy perception of God and one another, one must adjust one's thoughts and beliefs. Being a Christian, I understand the power of preventing one's thoughts from becoming harmful beliefs. I realize that when the same teachings are repeated continuously, those teachings arrest a person's thoughts, which themselves become what that person will meditate on. Whatever a person meditates on becomes what that person believes. Whatever one believes takes root in one's heart and then births the way in which one perceives and literally sees everything in life. What one believes is established mostly by what one is taught. This is why it so important that the perception of how men and women see God and one another is biblically clarified and taught according to the instructions that Jesus Christ left.

Although, I mentioned a few points about the Bible in the Introduction, I must share many more details about the Bible so that we understand the origin of the Bible itself, as well as the history of the model for relationships taught by most of the Christian church. To understand the origin of the history of the Christian perception of relationships between men and women, we must understand the history of the Bible both physically (i.e., how it was discovered and formed) and contextually (i.e., who wrote it and to whom it was written). I must explain both the physical and contextual aspects of the Bible so that the points I will be making about the teachings within the Christian church that impact the perception of males and females toward God and toward one another will make more sense throughout this book. To help those who may not know much about the Bible, let me take a few minutes to explain some details about it. The Bible is a compilation of books inspired by God and written by mortal men over an extended period of time. The books in the Bible were originally written in Hebrew, Aramaic, and Greek. Originally, the books were written more like letters (without chapters and verses) by men before, during, and after Christ. Over time, the Biblical writings fell into the hands of the Catholic Church and, after a while, chapters and verses were added. The actual physical books that became the Bible were selected by Catholic bishops, who determined the standard of what was divine and created a canon to maintain their selections. After the Reformation led by Martin Luther, the Christian Protestant Church broke away from the core standards of the Catholic Church. Therefore, the Catholics shared their canonized books with the Protestants. Today, the mainstream Christian Bible has 66 books while the Catholic Bible has 73. Using two different versions of the Bible – both the Protestant and the Catholic – can reveal each church's beliefs about following Jesus Christ. It has been noted and verified that other books of the Bible were found with and long after the selected books of the Bible were canonized. However, because the Catholic bishops did not deem all the other books to be divine and acceptable, no other books were added to the mainstream Bible.

Contextually, as a whole, the Bible is split into two parts that are shared between the Jews and the Christians. The Old

Testament was written to and for the Jews before Christ while the New Testament was written during and after Christ to those who followed and believed in Him. The Old Testament holds the Old Covenant, which consists of 613 Mosaic laws (also known as God's laws or commandments) that were given by God, initiated through circumcision by Abraham, and spoken to the Jews (also known as God's chosen people, Israelites, children of Israel, and the Hebrew people) through a man named Moses. Those commandments are split into three parts: ceremonial laws (consisting of the instructions for Jewish priests selected by God to present blood offerings in the Jewish temple), moral laws (the Ten Commandments), and civil laws (laws that instruct the order for relationships between men and women, how men and women should and should not dress, nutritional diets, how to treat the dead, etc.). Traditionally, the perception of male and female relationships has come from civil laws. These perceptions have been the standard for all Jewish relationships and the majority of non-Jewish relationships (Christian and non-Christian). Then the New Testament holds the New Covenant commandments that were instructed by God and implemented by His Son, Jesus Christ, who is also known as Yeshua and the Messiah. The commandments of Christ are supposed to be used to build the foundational beliefs of the Christian church. Although the Jews and the Christians have separate parts of the Bible, the only difference between them is how they perceive Jesus Christ. The Jews (whose religion is better known as Judaism) believe and follow only the Old Covenant Mosaic laws written in the Old Testament. They do not believe that their Savior is Jesus Christ, so they reject Jesus as their Messiah. In doing so, they reject the Christian New Testament. Therefore, the Jews are still waiting for their Messiah, who to the Christians is the Anti-Christ. Today, the Christians are waiting for the Second Coming of Jesus Christ, who is the only true Messiah and whom the Jews rejected the first time.

Hopefully, now we can clearly see and understand that both the Old and the New Testaments consist of different thought processes that form two different belief systems and perceptions of God. One perception is before Christ; the other is after Christ. Because the Christian church regards both the New and Old Testaments as being relevant to their teachings, I have found it imperative that when a Christian reads the Bible, that person reads it with a New Covenant Christ-centered perception. If the person doesn't, the book can take on a deadly and abusive turn. Due to an improper perception of the Bible, throughout history the mistreatment of women has been justified by many men who did not (and who do not) have a Christ-centered perception of God's character and heart.

Out of all relationships, the two that receive the most attacks in our perception is our relationship with God and individual relationships between men and women. Both the relationship between God and humanity and the relationship between men and women affect our marital relationships. Our perceptions of God, the opposite sex, and our spouses seem to be targeted by Satan the most. I know firsthand how the venom of Satan's deceptive plan of discord can attack a marriage. In my marriage, I was verbally and emotionally abused. Toward the end of my marriage, I feared physical violence. My husband created an environment that caused me to feel like I was less than a human being because I was a woman. I often felt like a second-class citizen and a prisoner in my own home. At times, due to my ex-husband's seared perception of God's heart behind His words, he blindly used specific scriptures to manipulate, control, and force me to do what he wanted me to do. Sadly, although the Bible gives great instructions about relationships, it is also one of the most misinterpreted books about relationships on the planet. I'm sure it has a quiet ranking as the number-one book in the world to be used to manipulate, control, and abuse people throughout history. Unfortunately, when men or women read the Bible devoid of God's heart and Christ perception, abuse of some sort will always take place. Consequently, women as a whole, especially those within the Christian church, have fallen prey to volatile men who misinterpret the Bible so that they can gain precedence over women and maintain a superior presence. They do all this while using the Bible as a means to justify their behavior.

Although I have not found specific statistics that state how many Christian marriages end due to domestic abuse, I believe that many Christian marriages end because of it. No matter how one perceives what I am saying, it is a fact that the Bible will always mean different things to different people. Perception is influenced by beliefs and is based on the presence of the Holy Spirit (or lack thereof), the heart of God through the revelation of Jesus Christ (or His absence), and the overall softness of a person's heart. In addition, the psychological and emotional health of a person will determine how they interpret the Bible. If you don't believe me, I encourage you to research cult leaders like Jim Jones, David Berg, and David Koresh. Each cult leader does not use the Bible for its intended purpose: to give life to those who hear it. Instead, cult leaders like those I mentioned use the Bible to manipulate and groom the minds of their victims so that they can use the Bible to justify a much more acceptable means of controlling people. We can also see how a false perception of God caused many Caucasian Christians to use the Bible to justify buying, selling, and enslaving millions of Africans for decades. Even a known hate group called the Ku Klux

Klan (KKK) had its roots in the Christian church. On the other hand, during the civil rights movement, a man named Martin Luther King Jr. used that same Bible to stop segregation and change the laws for African Americans once and for all. Even during Apartheid in South Africa, the Bible was used to promote and maintain segregation and division. Today, the Bible is still being used by people to debate the illegal immigration issue in America. Some say that illegal immigrants must be in America even if they don't follow the law, while others say that everyone, regardless of where they come from, must follow the law. In the end, both sides of the argument use the Bible to justify their beliefs. I can go on and on with stories throughout history that show how people who claimed to know God used the Bible to hurt, control, manipulate, abuse, hate, and enslave millions. Sadly, when a person (male or female) reads the Bible devoid of God's Holy Spirit, with self-centered beliefs and an emotionally seared or mentally distraught perception, that person will almost always end up falling short in self-love, abusing and oppressing someone, and living their whole life perceiving God through the eyes of a broken soul, peering through the fragmented pieces of misguided love.

CHAPTER 2

THE BREATH OF PERCEPTION

One day, a thought birthed belief and gave breath to perception. Perception is motivated solely by beliefs and based on what one thinks will determine what one believes in one's heart. The beliefs that are engraved in one's heart will determine that person's perception. Our beliefs are created by what we think about the most. What we meditate on in our thoughts will create our beliefs, and whatever we believe, we will live out in our actions every day. All relationships, especially our relationship with God and our marriage relationships, are dependent solely on the perception of what individual men and women think about one another and how men and women perceive God. So, as I mentioned in the Introduction, 100 percent of all relationships (such as the marriage relationship) are about perception. A marriage will be only as healthy as the beliefs that birth the perceptions toward it. The way in which a man and woman become one as husband and wife stems from how they both think and perceive one another individually as a man and as a woman. So, basically, it's not until our beliefs and thought processes confront and change our hearts, that our perception of the opposite sex will change; only then will the marriage relationship between husband and wife stand on a firm foundation, gain strength, and truly flourish.

If we imagine a relationship like a house, I guess our beliefs would be the foundation, our thoughts would be the walls, and our perception would be the windows. Every successful relationship must have vision and sight for the future. However, when our thoughts become blinded by dismantling beliefs and a blurry perception of God and the opposite sex, any relationship will experience a crack in its foundation. The walls will crumble and the windows will shatter. For example, if a husband perceives his wife as a habitual nag, it's highly possible that he will lose respect for her and hesitate to listen to her even if she has something valuable to say. The same goes for the woman—if a woman perceives her husband's actions as habitually harsh, most likely she will lose respect for him and not listen to or value what he says.

Perception Before the Fall

For us to understand the essence of the male and female relationship, we must go all the way back to Adam and Eve. At the beginning, before the fall of man, in the Book of Genesis, we see a clear vision and plan that God had for His human creation. God showed His heart of love when He gave the gift of choice and dominion over the earth to both male and female. Genesis 1:26-28 says, *"Then God said, 'Let Us make man in Our image, according to Our likeness; let them have dominion over the fish of the sea, over the birds of the air, and over the cattle, over all the earth and over every creeping thing that creeps on the earth.' So, God created man in His own image; in the image of God He created him; male and female He created them. Then God blessed them, and God said to them, 'Be fruitful and multiply; fill the earth and subdue it; have dominion over the fish of the sea, over the birds of the air, and over every living thing that moves on the earth.'"* These verses clearly show us that God gave both Adam and Eve the commandment to walk in dominion as equal partners on the earth, both having been made in His image together as one. He commanded them to be fruitful and multiply on the earth. Based on God's original vision for both men and women, we should clearly see that God did not give authority only to males, but to females as well. Also, we should notice that at no time before the fall did God give males preeminent authority over females and vice versa. Another thing to point out is in verse 26, where God said, *"Let Us make man in Our Image and let us make them have dominion"* ... If you notice, God used the plural form— "them"—to describe both male and female. One thing to note is that often, when God says "man," He is referring to male and female equally as a part of Him and as an equal part of one another. Within specific contexts throughout the Bible that describe humanity as a whole, the words "man" and "mankind" should be perceived as describing both male and female. However, this is not always the perception conveyed within most of the Christian church. For example, Genesis 2:8 and Genesis 2:15 say, *"The LORD God planted a garden eastward in Eden, and there He put the man whom He had formed." "Then the LORD God took the man and put him in the garden of Eden to tend and keep it."* Interestingly, there are many arguments within the Christian church that allude to the fact that before God created the woman, He gave complete dominion over all the earth to the male. However, we learned in Genesis 1:26-28 that this interpretation is far from the aligned perception of the overall reality of what actually happened. Most of the arguments do not truly reflect the chronological order that Genesis chapter 1 reveals. In that passage, we learned that God gave dominion over the earth to both male and female equally. It was there where He also gave the commandment to be fruitful and multiply on the earth. Now, my question is: If the concept conveyed by most of the Christian church (i.e., perceiving God as having placed Adam alone in the garden outside the evident timeline) is true…how can Adam be fruitful and multiply by himself? Contrary to popular belief, it is impossible for God to have placed Adam alone in the garden because a male and female cannot be fruitful and multiply on the earth apart from one another. In my opinion, considering the fact that God made male and female on the same day, the chronological timeline seems to be the biggest misperception. Also, once the collective terms "man" and "mankind" are understood, the Bible reads as being much more inclusive of both sexes. Equally, it makes a lot more sense for both women and men.

Some may say that because Genesis chapter 1 mentions the creation of both Adam and Eve, the description of "man" being placed in the garden, reflected in Genesis 2:8 and Genesis 2:15, technically should include Eve. I must say, I think those who perceive it that way have a point. However, regardless of how the timeline is perceived, God's overall original plan is clearly seen in the beginning, before the fall.

To God, it is evident that the female has dominion over the earth just as much as the male does.

The next argument that comes up a lot within the Christian church is: Because God made man first, men are supposed to be the predominant leaders. However, regardless of whether God created the male first and the woman second, He didn't command Adam to lead Eve, nor did He give Adam dominion over Eve. The fact is, a man cannot be fruitful by himself; nor can a female be fruitful by herself. One sex can never produce a human life without the other; to God, one sex cannot truly live in dominion without the other living in it as well. This is why God established a relationship between a man and a woman to include joint dominion and mutual submission, with each person standing together equally as one (Genesis 2:24—I will discuss more about God's original plan for marriage in Chapter 10).

Created for Relationship

Genesis 3:8 says, *"And they heard the sound of the LORD God walking in the garden in the cool of the day, and Adam and his wife hid themselves from the presence of the LORD God among the trees of the garden."* This verse tells me that God must have come down from heaven often and walked with Adam and Eve, speaking to them daily in the garden. I believe this verse is a glimpse into how close God was to both Adam and Eve before the fall. Although the verse is referring to what God did after the fall, to me it shows that God came down from heaven and personally spoke to Adam and Eve one on one. When Adam and Eve made the choice to disobey God, they hid from God and avoided communicating with Him. Because communication is one of the main bases for any relationship, they removed themselves from having a relationship with Him. To me, this verse paints a picture of God as one who came down from heaven to personally connect with Adam and Eve—as one who missed the presence of His son and daughter. Apparently, God came down from heaven on that particular day looking for Adam and Eve because He missed hearing their voices in the garden. God came down looking to find out exactly what happened to His family. To me, this verse shows a picture of the personal relationship God had with both Adam and Eve. God never had to go through Adam to approach Eve or vice versa.

It appears that, in the cool of the day, Adam and Eve walked with God often in the garden. They were close buddies—legitimate, trusting friends. So, as you can see, before the fall, Adam and Eve walked with God peacefully in the garden, with no ill thoughts about God or one another. Before the fall, the thought process of man was at peace, resting in God's peaceful vision for mankind and the whole earth. God loved and respected Adam and Eve; He perceived Adam and Eve as His son and daughter. Before the fall, Adam and Eve loved and respected God; they looked at and perceived God as their Father and their friend. Before the fall, Adam and Eve's perception of one another was respectful, honorable, and reflective of how they both loved themselves and God. Adam and Eve walked as one in a good, respectful, and honorable relationship. So, as we can see, before the fall, Adam and Eve perceived God and one another as a close-knit family, joined by love and respect for God's boundaries.

CHAPTER 3

THE ORIGIN OF MARRIAGE

In the beginning, the first two to be married were Adam and Eve. God saw Adam as a husband before Eve ever came along, and I'm sure God saw Eve as a wife long before she was introduced to Adam. Ultimately, it was that time at the very beginning when God gave all of mankind a glimpse of what He expected a relationship to look like. Long before there was a judge or minister to perform a marriage ceremony, there was a marriage between one man and one woman. So, in the beginning, without a ceremony and a piece of paper, what made a marriage a marriage? Apparently, a marriage is not a marriage until God calls it one. I have always believed that marriage should start in the heart of each person, long before two people ever stand in front of a judge or minister.

Long before a legal marriage takes place, as I said previously, marriage is all about how men and women think about one another and perceive one another in their hearts. If both male and female perceptions of one another are healthy before the legal marriage, then after the legal marriage, the male and female perceptions of one another will be more liberated, purposeful, and celebrated.

In Genesis 2:18, the Bible says, *"And the Lord God said, It is not good that the man should be alone; I will make a help meet for him."* In this verse, God introduced the concept of marriage. In Hebrew, the word "helpmeet" is "ezer," which means "a helper." In this verse, God announces His plans for marriage; man never planned marriage for himself. Basically, Adam was not the one who defined what marriage was; God did. Adam did not set the standard for marriage; God did. God had plans for His creation—plans that were clearly seen only before Adam and Eve ate of the forbidden fruit and fell under the same curses that, today, all of humanity still suffers from spiritually and psychologically.

The Curses of Adam and Eve

After the fall of man, everyone who participated in the disobedient action of eating the forbidden fruit was cursed. The curses that were placed by God affected the overall thought processes of both males and females. They also affected the overall image of the public forum of the Christian church. Satan received a curse that seems as if it literally changed his physical appearance and situated his thought process in a place where he would never connect with God— where, instead, he would always be at war with God and His people. Adam and Eve also received curses from God that manifested in the form of a lasting mental punishment described in Genesis chapter 3. In Genesis 3:14-15, God cursed Satan, while in Genesis 3:16-19, God cursed Adam and the Woman:

> *"So, the Lord God said to the serpent: 'Because you have done this, You are cursed more than all cattle, And more than every beast of the field; On your belly you shall go, And you shall eat dust All the days of your life. And I will put enmity Between you and the woman, And between your seed and her Seed; He shall bruise your head, And you shall bruise His heel.' To the woman He said: 'I will greatly multiply your sorrow and your conception; In pain you shall bring forth children; Your desire shall be for your husband, And he shall rule over you.' Then to Adam He said, 'Because you have heeded the voice of your wife, and have eaten from the tree of which I commanded you, saying, 'You shall not eat of it':*

'Cursed is the ground for your sake; In toil you shall eat of it All the days of your life. Both thorns and thistles it shall bring forth for you, And you shall eat the herb of the field. In the sweat of your face you shall eat bread Till you return to the ground, For out of it you were taken; For dust you are, And to dust you shall return.'

When Adam and Eve fell out of relationship with God, they no longer thought about God in the same way. Their thoughts about God—and about each other—changed. The verses above clearly shows us that after the fall, Adam immediately used God as a scapegoat, blaming Him for having created the woman. In Adam's mind, the woman and God were His enemies. Also, we can see how Eve used Satan as the scapegoat, blaming him for her disobedience to God's order. So, as we see right away, after the fall, Adam and Eve began to look at God as someone who was out to get them. They started to hide from God, living exposed to their nakedness. Their disobedience kidnapped their minds, blinded them to what they had once experienced with God and with one another. Their perceptions showed enmity toward God and one another. Once Adam and Eve began to think about God as their enemy, their belief about God changed; He was no longer a friend but a foe. Once their beliefs about God changed, their perception of God changed as well. After the fall, humanity lost its way. In response, God embarked on a journey spanning thousands of years—a journey to motivate humanity to change its mind and to perceive God as friend and Father again. Once God was viewed as a friend and Father, and not as a foe, the way in which men and women perceived one another would change as well.

Basically, when God cursed Eve with her desire being for her husband and making the man rule and take dominion over her, God recognized the anger in Adam toward Eve. God set him above her, in a place where he could never connect with her. Therefore, the woman was unable to connect with the man. Remember in Genesis 3:12, Adam blamed God for creating Eve as his wife. So, it was fitting for God to curse Adam with a thought process that caused Adam to perceive the male sex as being superior to the female sex. Thus arose the perception that males were set by God to be a divine form of leadership over the woman. The curse of Eve is harmful not just to the woman, but also to the man.

You are probably thinking, 'How does part of the curse that God placed on the woman act as a curse for the man and affect him negatively?' Before I answer that question, let's look at the curse that God put directly on Adam. Then I will show you how the curse God placed on Eve created the thought processes that led to how men and women perceive one another. In Genesis 3:17-19, which we previously read in this chapter, you can see that God cursed the ground on which Adam walked. God cursed Adam to live and eat in pain all the days of his life. Adam's hard work would produce thorns and thistles, and he would work by the sweat of his brow and eat of his bread all the days of his life.

As you can see, out of everyone who received a curse, Adam had the longest and most extensive one, lasting to the end of his life. Now I will show you how the curse of Eve negatively affected man. When God cursed the male sex to rule over the female, that was neither a compliment for men nor an honored privilege. When God cursed Eve, the mind of man was placed in a mental prison, barricaded by a thought process that exalted the male sex as being solely favored by God and celebrated as the superior divine image of God. This thought process regarded the male as the one whom God ordained to be the sole provider, leader, and protector of the female. The mind of the female perceived the male as being on the same level as God— as her leader, protector, and provider. Then, to add to Adam's dilemma, God put a curse directly on him, one that prevented him from seeing his need for God, that chained him to working to gain God's acceptance, and that left him enslaved to his own strength as a means of relieving himself from the weight of the curses resting upon him.

Now, I want to state that the same curses that affected Adam's perception of God also affected the woman's perception of God. However, the one curse spoken over Eve caused her sex to become inferior to the male—that is, the curse that is ever so evident today in male and female relationships. Basically, the curse spoken over Eve caused males to live in a superior state of mind and females to live in an inferior state of mind. It's no surprise that many women—both Christian and non-Christian—who think under the curse find themselves constantly feeling insecure, overlooked, and valued less than men. Many women seem to do everything in their power to prove their value as being equal to men. For many of us women, everything we do seeks to gain the attention of the superior male. We want him to want us and to think we are attractive. However, many of us who behave this way are continuously overlooked and never seen as good enough. This is because, due to the curse, many men maintain a "superior" thought process that can never be satisfied. So, each curse placed a divisive thought process between males and females; it is those inferior and superior thoughts that have left males and females living at opposite ends of the relationship spectrum. If you think about it, a person who has a superior attitude is tough to connect with and very hard to please. Truthfully, who really wants to be in a relationship with a dictator or someone who perceives themselves as better than you, superior to you, more valuable than you, smarter than you, above you, etc.? Superior and inferior thinking is the main reason why men and women have struggled with their perceptions of one another.

When a man thinks under the curse, pride leads his thoughts like a slave and drags him where it wants him to go. When pride rules a man's mind, it places demands on the way he thinks about and perceives God and women. Pride dictates how the one it traps should be approached; what they say is right, is right or what they say is wrong, is wrong. Pride exalts itself as being equal to God, as devoid of the need to be submissive to Him or anyone else. A prideful attitude places itself above an apology, above compassion for others, above empathy, above understanding, above self-respect, above one's own emotions, and above God's order. Pride exalts itself above others, never seeing itself as equal to anyone but as one to be served, not as one who serves. Pride always looks down on humility and calls it weak. Most of the time, pride causes a person with a superior perception in life to struggle in the emotional area, being unable to show or express emotions. The prideful mindset that originated from the curse of Eve basically sets the minds of many men in a superior, godlike state, thinking contrary to the humility that God intended for man. Men who habitually think and live under the curse are insecure and bound by pride. Often, to make themselves feel masculine and good about themselves, they must have their egos stroked by the women they rule over. Due to the curse, they find it challenging to grasp or see anything good within themselves, either emotionally or spiritually. This is the main reason why men who think under the curse rely solely on their wives for the home's spiritual and emotional stability. That curse prevents them from connecting with God. It also enslaves them to their physical work. A man's job has no soul, but with the thistles and thorns of loneliness, he is unable to maintain an emotional connection to God, himself, his wife, or his kids. Imagine living your whole life unable to connect with those closest to you on the same level of understanding. It is sad to see so many men—both Christian and non-Christian—who genuinely make efforts with their wives but who, due to how they think under the curse, live their whole lives like bystanders in their own homes. Many men sit in their homes, peering through the eyes of their cursed perception and watching their wives raise their children. Sadly, many men unknowingly live their lives under the weight of the curse of Eve. Bound by pride and due to the curse of Adam, they are separated from God and devoid of an antidote within themselves that will help them shake their superior perception of themselves. These are the perceptions that always seem to keep them at an emotional and spiritual distance from those they genuinely try so hard to love.

Adam and Eve vs. God

After the fall, man thought that God was at fault for creating woman, who disobeyed and coerced man into eating the forbidden fruit. In Genesis 3:12, it says, *"Then the man said, 'The woman whom You gave to be with me, she gave me of the tree, and I ate.'"* As you can see, Adam blamed God for the decision that Adam had made to willingly eat of the fruit that God had said "no" to. Initially, before the woman was pulled out of Adam, he had been given direct orders from God to not eat the fruit from the forbidden tree. However, when confronted by God about his behavior, Adam perceived God as the one to blame, for creating the woman who deceived him. Basically, as you can see, the fall caused man's thoughts and beliefs about God to change for the worse. Therefore, how man perceived God changed as well. From that moment on, God was thought of as an enemy and perceived to be against man.

The woman, on the other hand, did not blame God or Adam. Instead, she blamed the serpent for her actions. In Genesis 3:13, it says, *"And the Lord God said to the woman, 'What is this you have done?' The woman said, 'The serpent deceived me, and I ate.'"* Here, we see how the Woman blamed the serpent (representing Satan) for being the one who made her eat of the forbidden fruit. If the Woman perceived the serpent as being the reason for her actions, that would mean she thought of Satan's influence over her as being stronger than that of God. Therefore, the woman's actions reflect disrespect and disregard for the instructions that God had given her. One thing I want to point out is that once a person is thought of negatively, that person is no longer perceived respectfully. Because love and respect are formed together and cannot be separated, when a person loses respect, the perception of what love looks like will fade away as well.

Women vs. Men

The battle of the sexes started in the garden with Adam and Eve and has gone on for centuries. Which sex is stronger—male or female? Which sex is smarter—male or female? How is it that two species that once walked as one could become so competitive, cold, and harsh toward one another? How is it that two species created in God's image could be raised to focus more on their differences than on their similarities? What must we do to change our perception of one another? Where do we start?

Well, as you read previously, man blamed God and the woman for his decision to disobey God. From that point on, not only was man's relationship with God broken, but his perception of God was destroyed. His relationship with the woman was broken and destroyed as well. So, I would say that the battle of the sexes began in the garden. The reality is, instead of taking responsibility for and being honest about his actions, Adam chose to condemn God and the woman for his decision to follow the woman and disobey God. Truthfully, until the way men and women think about one another changes, their perceptions of one another will never change.

As a matter of fact, within the Christian church today, the male sex is somehow perceived as the only one created in God's image. However, what's interesting is that before the fall, as Genesis 1:26-28 clearly states, male and female were both created in God's image. That verse never said that only males hold the image of God. Both male and female were created in the image of God. We also saw that God never gave dominion of the woman to the man, He gave dominion only over the earth and any non-human species on it, and He gave this dominion to both the male and the female, not just the male. Yet, as we proceed, we will discover that within most of the Christian church, men and women are taught to perceive themselves in a manner contrary to God's original plan before the fall. Therefore, what we will discover are the same fallen perceptions that began in the garden—the perceptions that men and women have of God and of one another. These perceptions exist in the vast majority of Christian churches today.

Satan's Plan

The first thing Satan did in Genesis chapter 3 was to influence the division not just between God and man, but between Adam and Eve. Satan aimed to destroy the core of unity between a man and a woman. His first weapon was an attack on God's order for relationships. In Genesis 3:1-7, we read about all the events that led man to fall into the cycle of sin.

"Now the serpent was more cunning than any beast of the field which the Lord God had made. And he said to the woman, 'Has God indeed said, 'You shall not eat of every tree of the garden'?' And the woman said to the serpent, 'We may eat the fruit of the trees of the garden; but of the fruit of the tree which is in the midst of the garden, God has said, 'You shall not eat it, nor shall you touch it, lest you die.'' Then the serpent said to the woman, 'You will not surely die. For God knows that in the day you eat of it your eyes will be opened, and you will be like God, knowing good and evil.' So when the woman saw that the tree was good for food, that it was pleasant to the eyes, and a tree desirable to make one wise, she took of its fruit and ate. She also gave to her hus-

*band with her, and he ate. Then the eyes of both
of them were opened, and they knew that they
were naked; and they sewed fig leaves together
and made themselves coverings."*

As you can see, Satan showed up with only one agenda— to destroy God's original order for all relationships. After Adam and Eve ate the fruit and realized that their nakedness was exposed, Adam immediately blamed God for giving him Eve as his wife. Adam then placed all responsibility on Eve, as if she were the one who "forced" him to eat the forbidden fruit (Genesis 3:12). Then the woman blamed Satan, as if he had "forced" her to eat the forbidden fruit (Genesis 3:13). Other than what Satan did, Adam and Eve both deceived themselves, denying the fact that they had both chosen to eat the forbidden fruit. A vast majority of Christian churches teach that Eve received her instructions about the forbidden fruit from her husband, Adam. As a matter of fact, in Genesis 2:16-17 it says, *"And the LORD God commanded the man, saying, 'Of every tree of the garden you may freely eat; but of the tree of the knowledge of good and evil you shall not eat, for in the day that you eat of it you shall surely die.'"* In these verses, it appears as though God addressed Adam as if He had a relationship only with Adam. This would exclude Eve from the equation.

However, as we learned earlier, God created both male and female in His own image on the same day. Also, as we read previously, He gave them both dominion over the earth and gave neither one dominion over the other. In addition, we learned that, often, when the word "man" is used, God is referring to both male and female as a whole. What I have discovered is that when I read the Bible before I learned how to see God through Christ perception, I did so using the perception of the curses of Adam and Eve. Truthfully, whenever any part of the Bible is read outside the perception of Jesus Christ, the only other perception that remains is veiled by Adam and Eve's dysfunctional thoughts. In general, it seems that when people read the Bible blinded by Adam and Eve's thought process, they somehow always dismiss or downplay the liberation that God gave to the woman. Of course, the perception that males are favored by God and were established by God as the superior sex, intended to lead the female, is completely contrary to God's complete vision for both men and women. This concept is a misperceived notion that really does not align with God's heartfelt desire and overall plan to have a direct relationship with both male and female, whom He created equally in His image.

Once God's original plan for relationships is understood, we will see clearly that it is impossible for God to have gone through Adam to approach Eve. We will discover that God created both male and female so that they would each have a direct relationship with Him, as He is the only one who leads, covers, protects, and provides for them both. God is the one who gave the earth and the garden to both male and female as a gift. Neither Adam nor Eve provided anything. So, in reality, neither Adam nor Eve was the provider; instead, God reigned as the sole provider. Adam and Eve both received the earth as a gift from God. The gift of the earth was accompanied with dominion over the earth, which God gave to them both. With that reality being understood, why would God declare that both male and female had been created equal in His image and then turn around and go through Adam to relay His instructions to Eve? Consequently, contrary to popular belief, God did not go through Adam to convey His instructions to Eve. What you will find as we journey further is that God's original plan was not in agreement with the order for relationships that came after the fall. Unfortunately, it is that fallen order that most doctrines within the Christian church convey. In Genesis 3:1 above, we see in the underlined portion that Satan clearly said, "Has God indeed said." He did not say, "Has Adam indeed said." The instructions to not eat from the forbidden tree were directly from God and delivered to both the woman and the man.

However, today, most of the Christian church teaches that, from the beginning, women rebelled against the instructions given by Adam the first husband. The reality is that both Adam and Eve were individually created to have direct access to God. The woman did not have to go through Adam to approach God and obtain His instructions. As I mentioned before, some people speculate that the verses were placed out of proper chronological order and, consequently, that Eve was physically pulled out of Adam much sooner than the timeline appears to conclude. In other words, Eve was in Adam when the instructions were given. Either way, one can conclude that Adam and Eve were one unit joined by God. It's just like how a child within a womb can hear his or her parents' voices and even listen to and understand the sound of music. In essence, even if the chronological order as written is correct and Eve was in existence within Adam when God handed down His instructions, Eve was still able to hear directly from God. So, in my opinion, no matter how you look at it, when Adam received the instructions directly from God, so did the woman.

In reality, human life cannot be birthed into existence without an intimate connection between one man and one woman. Once we understand this connection, we can clearly see how both the male and the female are valuable treasures to God. Only His order can preserve and protect them. Because a woman is the carrier of life, her relevance to God is equal to that of the man. A man can donate his sperm, but without a woman's eggs and womb, that sperm will never produce life. A woman can donate her eggs, but without sperm, no life can be produced. Simply by knowing that, we can see that God created men and women to fit together like a glove over a hand. However, Satan's influence on the perceptions of men and women has caused division and created a war between the sexes. Because God's heart and vision for men and women are to build the family unit, Satan's ultimate plan is to destroy God's vision for that family unit. The war that Satan influenced has left an undeniable mark of separation and discord between men and women. Unknowingly, the doctrines within the Christian church have conveyed and upheld that mark. Sadly, after the fall, the essence of the unity intended between men and women was lost, and the plan that Satan introduced to destroy God's vision for relationships between God and humanity and between males and females took precedence throughout history. Within that plan, some men have become oppressors, veiled by the curse of Eve and using the Bible to rule over women. Sometimes those men become physically, emotionally, or verbally abusive toward women, all in the name of God.

CHAPTER 4

THE ROAD TO ABUSE

Today, one of the biggest and most harmful issues for any woman is being in a relationship with an abusive man. More than one term is used to describe domestic abuse; "domestic violence" and "intimate partner violence" are also phrases used to represent it. Abuse is like a moving car with child-proof locks. Once a person gets into the car, they need help getting out. In my analogy, the car is the relationship, the driver is usually the abuser, and the abused is the one sitting on the passenger's side, locked in. As long as the abuser is driving the car, the abused will never feel safe emotionally, spiritually, mentally, physically, or psychologically.

Marriage is not the only place to find an abuser; they also appear in engaged couples, boyfriend/girlfriend relationships, and other areas within society as a whole, including some public areas of the Christian church. No matter where an abuser is found, what they do to people is the same. An abuser abuses. An abuser would not be an abuser if they did not have poisonous beliefs that birthed abusive behaviors and destructive attitudes toward another person, especially a romantic interest. Unlike the other relationships, a legal marriage can act as a locked prison for some, while for others it can be an open space with boundary lines. I say this because once a couple commits to a legal marriage, getting out of that relationship is a lot more complicated, especially if the couple has children. To dissolve a marriage in the courts takes time and a lot of paperwork. Basically, dissolving a marriage is a legal matter; marriage isn't something you can walk out of. Therefore, when abuse occurs in a marriage relationship, the abused person can feel trapped economically, physically, psychologically, and legally.

Before we go any further, let me take a minute to answer the question: What is abuse? According to vocabulary.com, "The word abuse is made up of two parts

—'use,' which means to employ, and ab-, a Latin prefix meaning 'away' — and as a whole comes from the Latin abūsus, meaning 'misuse,' or 'use wrongly.'" So, abuse basically occurs when a person misuses a human life in a way that deviates from God's intention. God did not intend for a person to control, manipulate, or seek to have power over another person.

Did You Know?

Both women and men experience abuse. Sometimes society overlooks the issue of the abuse of men. According to statistics taken from cdc.gov and ncadv.org, both women and men suffer from intimate partner violence:

- On average, nearly 20 people per minute are physically abused by an intimate partner in the United States. In one year, this equates to more than 10 million women and men.

- 1 in 3 women and 1 in 4 men have been victims of some form of physical violence by an intimate partner within their lifetime.

- 1 in 4 women and 1 in 7 men have been victims of severe physical violence by an intimate partner in their lifetime.

- On a typical day, more than 20,000 phone calls are placed to domestic violence hotlines nationwide.

- Intimate partner violence accounts for 15% of all violent crimes.

- Women between the ages of 18-24 are most commonly abused by an intimate partner.

- 19% of domestic violence involves a weapon.

- Domestic victimization is correlated with a higher rate of depression and suicidal behavior.

The Different Forms of Domestic Abuse

There are many different forms of domestic abuse. Other than what I have discovered from research, several forms on the list below were taken from educational material about domestic abuse, published by an organization called Hope Alliance in Round Rock, TX. It covers many, but not all forms. Each form has specific characteristics. However, for the sake of the topic of this book, we will be discussing only two forms of abuse underlined in the list below:

- Physical violence

- Emotional/Verbal abuse

- Sexual assault

- Religious abuse

- Sexism

- Financial economic abuse

When it comes to the Christian church or society in general, although all forms of abuse may be present, in some cases the two forms that I believe receive the most momentum due to the way in which some people within the Christian church interpret the Bible are sexism and religious abuse.

My Life with an Abuser

When I was going through my situation, I had no idea what to call it. All I knew was that I was emotionally punished, yelled at, and insulted a lot. No matter what I did to make my marriage work, my former husband was not willing to do what was needed to change our thoughts or perceptions of one another. Instead, he used the Bible to put fear in me, to keep me in the relationship and prevent me from leaving or having a voice. When I called the domestic abuse hotline, I learned what abuse was. Only then did I realize that I was in an abusive domestic situation. When I went through counseling and attended support groups, I learned that the Christian church does not always welcome the information that domestic abuse organizations provide. The staff at the organization assisting me through my transition out of my marriage informed me that they had tried to make efforts with the local Christian church in central Texas, but they had never been invited in. They told me that a gap existed between domestic violence education and the Christian church.

Within the general society, many women and men suffer abuse directly without a Bible. However, within the Christian church, many men use the Bible like a mask that covers their abusive ways. Although domestic abuse is part of society as a whole, the Christian church rarely discusses it publicly due to

how the Bible is perceived in regard to male and female relationships. Sadly, many Christians do not have a voice when it
comes to abuse that takes place within some Christian marriages. In general, many people in the Christian church are
not exposed to the world of domestic abuse until they experience it personally. That was basically my story. I was not
aware of what domestic abuse was until I experienced it myself.

As a Christian, growing up I was encouraged and taught
to date and choose a mate based on my faith in God. When I
chose my husband, I was not aware of how a man can use the
Bible as a tool to manipulate and control a woman. Before
entering the world of domestic abuse, I had no idea what
domestic abuse really was. I thought it was only physical in
nature. I had no idea it was also verbal and emotional. Although I grew up in a home where emotional and verbal domestic abuse was present, I was not aware of that fact at the
time. It was not until I went through my own situation that I
learned what abusive behavior was. I did not realize that the
screaming, disrespect, and insults common within my child-
hood environment were actually considered domestic abuse.
Sadly, domestic abuse or abusive behaviors were barely identified or discussed in my home. After I started learning about
my situation and discovered that the same behavior had been
part of my home life when I was a child, I discovered that my

mother herself had grown up in an abusive domestic environment, suffering abuse at the hands of her stepfather.

So, there I was, in a marriage that was failing due to domestic abuse and suddenly realizing that abusive environments had been a part of my life as far back as I could remember. Apparently, if we sit in a specific situation long enough, we can become so comfortable that those toxic environments become familiar places to live.

The saddest thing is that church attendance was at the core of every situation and the reading of the Bible was prevalent. My mother saw abusive behavior throughout her life as well. Surprisingly, she had been raised in a home where church attendance was mandatory for her and her siblings. When I was growing up, my mom and stepdad made attending Sunday morning church services mandatory for me and my younger brothers. After I grew up and got married, I believed in attending Sunday morning services and upholding the standards of the Bible as I had been taught. Yet, in every situation I mentioned, domestic abuse existed. In my family, I discovered three generations of abusive behaviors that went unnoticed and that were never identified as domestic abuse...until my marriage crashed and burned because of it. If one does not know that a problem exists, how can that problem be corrected? If a person is comfortable in harsh, volatile environments, the chances of that person changing and transitioning out of a harmful environment, into a healthier environment are slim to none. Consequently, although my failed marriage hurt, God used it to help me see that the biggest pitfall in my marriage had been what the Christian church had taught me to believe about relationships.

CHAPTER 5

SEXISM AND RELIGIOUS ABUSE

To learn more about the two areas of domestic abuse that affect more Christian marriages, we must detail what they are. Other than my own research and interpretation, some information from the list below is from Hope Alliance, located in Round Rock, Texas.

What Is Sexism?

- Discrimination based on male or female sex.

- Using the belief that the male sex is superior to females, or that males have certain privileges that females should not have, to justify being a controlling partner.

- The male is usually the one who defines male and female roles.

- The male is expected to make all the big decisions without input from the female partner.
- The male sets rules for the relationship that are not the same for both partners.

What Is Religious Abuse?

- Men who use the Bible illegally to force a woman into submission.
- A man or woman who uses the Bible or any other religious book to control, manipulate, and place fear into another to do what they want to be done. This also goes for a religious leader who abuses his or her authority by putting an unhealthy fear of God in people by using the Bible to manipulate, control, or abuse their congregants to do what they want or need to be done.
- Men who use the Bible as an excuse for not respecting their wives or partners by saying, "Well, since the Bible does not tell me to respect my wife, I don't have to," but who then demands respect from women because the Bible says that women "have" to respect men.
- Women who use the Bible as a means to force their husbands to love them.

We now know and understand the two areas of domestic abuse used most by some men within the Christian church.

How Are These Two Forms Used?

Any man is capable of using these two forms of abuse. Also, any woman is capable of using the Bible to abuse a man. However, the most prevalent verses in the Bible are used by many Christian men to abuse and oppress women. Sexism and religious abuse were the two forms of abuse that I found had a direct connection to almost all religious communities, including Christianity. Usually, religious abuse goes far beyond intimate relationships within religious communities and spills over into the culture of places of worship. It is seen mostly in the behavior of some religious leaders toward congregants.

When I started research, I found that domestic abuse is also a prevalent issue within the Muslim community. Some in the Muslim faith have established domestic abuse organizations to help their peers transition out of violent domestic situations. I have also discovered that many women in the Amish community are victims of domestic violence and that some of them have banded together to establish domestic abuse organizations that help their peers transition out of abusive relationships within that community. However, when I began to look up Christian organizations dedicated to Christians who suffer from domestic abuse, I did not find as many as I had expected. A few are out there, but not as many as I assumed it would be. To focus attention on the domestic abuse that takes place within the Christian church, I developed an organization called "Empowering Christians to Overcome Abuse (empoweringchristians.org)." This organization is aimed at offering informative resources and spiritual support to Christian women who have been or are currently in an abusive domestic relationship. Apparently, within the Christian church, the topic of domestic abuse is seldom addressed. However, I hope that my experiences as a Christian, coupled with the information in this book, will help many of us within the Christian church be more aware of the toxic doctrines and perceptions that are unknowingly projected onto many men and women.

Is God Sexist?

Well, based on what we read in the Bible in both the Old and New Testaments, it appears that God is just that: a sexist. I mean, when you look at the facts about women within the Bible, especially in the Old Testament, it does seem like women are somewhat blacklisted. The Old of polygamy and laws that make women look as if we are objects intended to be tossed back and forth by men. In the Old Testament, it appears as though the men showed little to no respect for women. They also had multiple wives and concubines. It seems as if God gave men a free pass to take women at their leisure, as long as they made their choices based on what God commanded. It seems like the Old Covenant contains more laws based on the sin and redemption of a woman than on the sin and redemption of a man. The first five books of the Bible are called the Torah. The first order of God was written within those books and carried out by Abraham and Moses. As I explained previously, in Chapter 1, the 613 commandments were written according to God's former order. These commandments gave the Jews specific instructions regarding what God considered to be a sin, the punishment for sin, and ways to be redeemed from sin. The Book of Leviticus details many of the Mosaic laws in the Old Covenant. In Leviticus 21:7 and Leviticus 21:14, God gave instructions to male priests, telling them whom they could and could not marry. If a woman was divorced, a prostitute, or even a widow, she was limited in terms of what she could do and whom she could marry. Here are a couple of verses that detail what God instructed male priests to do back then:

> *"They shall not take a wife who is a harlot or a defiled woman, nor shall they take a woman divorced from her husband; for the priest is holy to his God."*

> *"A widow or a divorced woman or a defiled woman or a harlot—these he shall not marry; but he shall take a virgin of his own people as a wife."*

Do you notice the double standard found within these two verses? Why is it that women were not told to avoid marrying a man who was a widower, divorced, or defiled? You can see from just these two verses alone how biased God's perception of women appears to be. It seems like throughout the Old Testament, men were allowed to get away with a lot more than women were. The only sins both males and females appeared to be called out on were murder, same-sex relationships, bestiality, etc. I know there were more sins than those, but I'm just using them to show that women were the primary targets for redemption in a vast majority of the Mosaic laws. Check out these verses in Numbers 5:29-31:

> *"This is the law in cases of jealousy, when a wife, though under her husband's authority, goes astray and defiles herself, or when the spirit of jealousy comes over a man and he is jealous of his wife. Then he shall set the woman before the Lord, and the priest shall carry out for her all this*

law. The man shall be free from iniquity, but the woman shall bear her iniquity."

By the looks of this verse, as I have said, based on a reading of many of God's redemptive laws toward women within the Old Covenant, it seems as if women were the primary individuals requiring redemption.

Regardless of whether you are a man or a woman, the manner in which God viewed women in the Old Testament seems evident. Considering this pattern in the Bible, it should be no surprise that even today, society still perceives women the same way—as lifeless trophies and mere second-class citizens, objects created to be ruled, bought, and sold by men. It seems like today men are still allowed to get away with a lot more than women are. Many people today still perceive that God excuses superior behavior from men and still punishes women for what Eve did. However, some people see God as One who excuses the bad behavior of certain men. Some Christian men who behave this way are not honestly looking at relationships according to the original order that God intended. There is a much deeper meaning behind the portrayal of women in the Old Testament. I will not use this book to detail the true spiritual symbolism behind the biblical image of a woman. However, in the future, I will release another book that dives into the deeper spiritual mystery of what the biblical image of the woman truly represents.

The Valley of Religious Abuse

Religious abuse within the public forum of the Christian church is such an important issue that I should probably dedicate an entire chapter to it. Actually, I should probably dedicate a whole book to it. Religious abuse is a widespread form of abuse within any faith-based community. Any time someone uses the Bible or any other religious book to oppress someone, put fear in someone, or force someone's obedience, that is considered religious abuse. Religious abuse is even worse for the Christian church because of the standards of Christ's liberated love that the church is supposed to represent. To me, in the Christian church, religious abuse extends far beyond intimate relationships. It invades the culture of the public forum of the Christian Church environment as a whole. Sadly, sometimes within the Christian circle, Christian leaders have been known to use the Bible to control, manipulate, and place fear in congregants. Many leaders do this in the hopes of scaring congregants into obeying what they say God wants instead of obeying what Jesus actually asked for. However, because this book is more about women breaking free from male oppression and about women's intimate relationships with God and their spouses, I won't address the other forms of religious abuse at this time.

Obligation Vs. Liberation

In a marriage relationship, the people in the marriage make a choice to marry. Each person has a free will and technically, other than the legal bonds they are responsible for upholding, the only ideals that keep a marriage together are found in what I call the seven pillars of a true Christ-centered relationship. Those pillars are communication, honesty, humility, love, respect, transparency, and trust. The reason why religious abuse is so dangerous is because it is wrong to use the Bible to "force" someone to do (or not do) something. I can tell you that, based on the way in which relationships are taught within the Christian church, the essence of what Jesus did and represented has been forgotten. The reality is when Jesus came, He liberated us so that we now have a choice. If we do what He commanded, we are to do so because we choose to love Him, not because we are afraid of Him and feel forced to love Him. So, according to Christ's standards of love, a husband should willingly choose to love his wife because he wants to, not because he "has" to. By the same token, a wife should willingly choose to love her husband because she wants to, not because she "has" to. A wife should not be forced to submit, and a husband should not be forced to love. A relationship rooted in obligation is created through force and exempt from free will. It will never exude sincere love, joy, or true liberation. On the other hand, when a relationship is rooted in a person's free will to choose, that choice will bring forth an abundance of sincere love, joy, and true liberation. The perception of liberation in a relationship will always be greater and stronger, and will produce a greater abundance of joy, than the perception of obligation ever will. My former husband used specific verses in the Bible to force me into submission. During that time, I experienced religious abuse and learned the difference between an obligated and liberated perception of love.

CHAPTER 6

BROKEN PERCEPTION

When we read the Bible, we must understand that it is not just a spiritual book. It is also a history book that shares the history of the origin of humanity as well as the history of the universe. It shows the history of the Jews and the Christians, and the history of God's appearance throughout time. The Bible also paints a picture of God's character and His intentions toward humanity. Yet, wrapped up in all the history of the Bible is the life-changing story of a man named Jesus Christ (Yeshua, Messiah, Emmanuel). Overall, the Bible is a beautiful book full of wonderful words wrapped in God's heart and delivered to man. Although the Bible was written with the valiant purpose of giving us a map back to God's heart, due to the disobedient actions of humanity we have trampled the essence of God's purpose. In our inability to connect with God's heart behind His words, some of us will abuse others and use God's name illegally to do so.

One factor that causes the most confusion about the Bible is how a person thinks about what they are reading. If a person thinks contrary to how God thinks, the chances of that person's perception of God's word being in alignment with God's heart and perception do not exist. If a person reads the Bible with preconceived ideas about what God expects, that person will misinterpret God's heart every time. I have also found that a person's emotional state can alter the way in which that person thinks about God and perceives His word. As I mentioned previously, when it comes to gender issues between men and women, it's all about the thought process. The issues between the sexes hinge on how men and women believe God thinks about and perceives them. The source of these perceptions will determine how men and women think about each other. Unfortunately, false perceptions are created when both sexes misunderstand and misperceive God's expectations of them. Sadly, due to our faulty perception of God's word, abusive behaviors within the Christian church have run rampant. Abusive behaviors are often excused and overlooked. They tend to take precedence as the perception of love. That broken perception of love cancels out the truth of what God actually and sincerely expects from all relationships.

Domestic Abuse Lives Under the Curses

Consider the fall of Adam and Eve, and the understanding of how both males and females think under the curses, This is the main reason why statistics show that more men abuse women than vice versa. Due to humanity's fallen nature, men and women are basically born to perceive one another through a thought process rooted in the curse spoken over Eve. Due to the curse of Adam, humanity is enslaved to a thought process that perceives God as our enemy and that separates us from Him. While thinking under the curse of Adam, we are imprisoned by a thought process that causes us to believe we must do good things to gain God's attention, acceptance, blessings, and salvation. In the overall status of society, living under the curses of Adam and Eve is a normal and very familiar part of life for everyone. Truthfully, Jesus Christ is the only One who was given rights by God to break these vicious thought patterns that create our beliefs and distort our perceptions of God and the opposite sex.

Unfortunately, even within the Christian church, abuse of women happens all the time. Often, because the Bible is misperceived and used to validate the superiority of men, abusive behavior remains unaddressed, unacknowledged, and uncorrected. When the original plan that God intended for His creation is not taught correctly, people have no idea who they are, and the dark, cold, desolate world of domestic violence continues to claim victims on both sides. The male abuser is trapped by a superiority complex and lives enslaved by the thought that God created his gender to rule over a woman as if the man were equal to God. Sadly, any man who believes his gender is superior to that of women will, in some way, become abusive and live his whole life seeking power and control over a woman, his children, or anyone else within his grasp.

Worship of the Alpha Male

In our society, men are inadvertently exalted and worshipped as divine gods. As women we are taught from a young age to serve a man respectfully and do everything for him. In addition, within the Christian church, it seems as if we are unintentionally taught to worship the man as if God had created him to be a symbol of God's divine nature. Because men are the predominant spiritual leaders within the Christian church, many of them have misinterpreted the Bible, depicting themselves as being literally superior to women and equal to the divinity of God. Unfortunately, within the Christian church, some male leaders misinterpret what it means to be made in God's image before the fall and have conveyed a message that exalts the fallen nature of man as being on the same level with God. By doing so, they create an image of the male sex as being superior divine beings whom God has called to serve as the sole life forms reflecting His image on earth. In reality, when one thinks about the image of God, one should think all-powerful, all-knowing, one who is in total control, one who is to be obeyed, revered, and respected, the only one to be worshiped. Consequently, within the Christian church, the very attributes we use to describe the nature of God have been inadvertently projected onto men. Based on specific Bible passages that we will cover later, it is as if women within the Christian church are taught that the nature of God is reflected more in men than in women, as if males really are equal to God. I don't think that most Christians realize their doctrines literally teach that men are to be revered as divine gods who are superior to women. Not only have women—both inside and outside the Christian church—been taught to innocently support men, but it appears to me that they have been unwittingly taught to worship men as gods, as men are the ones whom God uses to rule over women. Consequently, many men within the Christian church have been taught that women exist for only three reasons—to fulfill men's sexual needs and desires, to have men's babies, and to serve men as their helpmates, just as Eve was the helpmate to Adam. Although the teaching about women being helpmates seems innocent and scripturally sound, if the concept of being a helpmate is not taught from God's heart through the perception of Christ, the entire concept and goal of a relationship become one-sided—on the side of the male. Sadly, one-sided beliefs like this cause so many rifts in relationships between men and women within the Christian church. Because many Christian doctrines are veiled by the fallen thought process rooted in the curse of Eve, those teachings have influenced and affected the standards for relationships throughout the world. Sadly, because the one- sided perception veiled by the curse of Eve rules throughout the Christian church, the true essence of the two joined hearts that God created is never thought about, believed, or perceived.

When a mortal man perceives himself as one whom God "created" to be worshiped, respected, and revered by women, as one who has been given total control and power over women, failure in a relationship is imminent. Once a man upholds this perception, that man removes himself from a place of humble submission under God and puts himself at the same level as God, lording himself over another human being as though he were a god. Sadly, once any man perceives himself as superior and placed by God to rule over women, he will subconsciously start excusing his lustful, disrespectful behavior and his misguided actions toward women, without apologizing to women and without repenting to God. If a man perceives himself as next to God, as placed by God as superior to women, why would he apologize to women or to God for behaving in a way that he has been taught is just his "created nature"? In a relationship, beliefs like this cause men to stumble into pride and live their entire lives emotionally barren, prevented from ever having a healthy relationship with God or being able to connect with women on an equal emotional level. The perceptions under the curse are why so many men, both inside and outside the Christian church, struggle with faithfulness. A man who thinks under the curse can easily harden his emotions and live selfishly, disregarding his own conscience. One thing to note is that a man who thinks he is equal to God is numb to his own human emotions and cannot connect emotionally with another human being, especially the woman he says he loves. A man who perceives himself as a divine god cannot serve or think about anyone else but himself and about anything else but his own overwhelming need for sexual gratification and self-approval.

I don't want to be the bearer of bad news, but when a man perceives himself as a divine god, superior to a woman, that man sets himself on a self-destructive course. He basically places himself within the corridors of God's wrath, to be judged as an oppressor. Men blinded by the "I am a god" mentality always seem to place themselves and their work above God and their emotional connection to their families.

They also seem to use the profit from their "work" as a means of excusing their emotional and spiritual absence from their families. For instance, how many times has a man worked hard to support his family, yet he has no emotional connection to that family and never offers spiritual comfort in any way. Still, he is exalted as the "god" of his home solely based on his manhood and the physical provision he supplies to his family. The real God not only provides for His people, but He is a gentleman. He also has a heart-to-heart, emotional, and spiritual connection to His people. So, in reality, how is it possible for the Christian church to teach doctrines that exalt and place men (including abusive men) on a level equal to that of God? If their fallen nature is forever stained with sin, how can they come anywhere near the divine superior level of the Holy God to whom they are compared?

The fact is, we live in a world where one God sets the rules, and He has shown Himself to be loving and perfect in all His ways. However, due to the curse of Eve, the oppressive behaviors of many men toward women throughout history have shown that their very nature is far from perfect and that their image looks nothing like God. Technically, both males and females have disobeyed God's instructions from the beginning. Based on the initial fall into which Adam and Eve led humanity, we can see that men will never qualify as perfect, nor will a mortal man ever be equal to God on any level. God created both male and female to love and serve Him by humbly loving and serving one another equally. This is probably why the Woman "served" Adam the forbidden fruit that they both shared.

The Roots of Abuse

I believe that, to God, an abuser's heart is like a long, dark road that only the light emanating from Christ can brighten and change. Because abusive behaviors are rooted in the curse of Eve, women wage war against men as well. Sometimes, women desire to fight men naturally, as a way of over-ruling a man's cursed perception of women. In reality, no matter how one tries to stop being abusive, that person will not succeed until he changes how he thinks about himself. There is no other option for freedom but to change from the inside out. I have found that abusive behaviors are based on many factors, including how a person is raised, what a person experienced as a child, or sometimes poor emotional choices made as an adult. Technically, in my opinion, any person has the potential to become an abuser. However, the best candidates to embrace abusive behaviors are those who have a poor self-image and who do not love themselves.

I believe that anyone who habitually engages in abusive behaviors and yet speaks the name of Jesus is devoid of God's heart and character. Therefore, a man's habitual abusive actions and behavior reflect the fact that he does not have a true relationship with God. I have discovered that for God to get to the heart of a man blinded by the curses of Adam and Eve, that man must have a revelation about his need for God. A man must first see himself as a sinner who needs a Savior. If an abusive man never sees the need to change, why would that man seek God for freedom? Once a man sees that he has been created to have a relationship with God, he will see the need to think and meditate on the character of God, which is captured in the essence of His words. We must realize that it is God's Holy Spirit that illuminates God's character through His words, which transform a man's life so that it resembles what he is meditating on. Then and only then can a man see himself become the person whom God created him to be. The bondage of an abusive man is the bars of pride and a lack of self-love. Control and manipulation are the stamina that motivates an abusive man to dominate his victim. Once his victim is dominated, she becomes entrapped by fear and is afraid to leave him.

For God to get a hold of an abuser, He must confront the abuser about being honest regarding why he is choosing to be abusive. As the light of God's truth shines forth within that man, the roots of his abusive behavior are exposed. Then, once the man recognizes his own fear and lack of self-love, he will see how much pain he has caused. He will discover God's need to change him. Only then will he truly change. Sometimes, to truly confront and change his thought patterns, an abusive man may need to seek outside counsel. An outside source can help an abusive person discover the thought patterns that imprison his mind and that cause him to abuse the one he says he loves. In reality, these truths about abusers should be applied to females who abuse men as well.

God's Heart Abhors Abuse

In Chapter 1, I clarified the three parts of the 613 commandments from the Old Testament. So now, it should be easier to understand that once Christ came and established a new perception of God, the image of God that once appeared to paint a negative perception of women (which I addressed in Chapter 5) is no longer acceptable. Christ came and established a different perception of God, one that reflected His loving heart and gentle character of love, peace, grace, and mercy. God no longer accepts the perception of men who believe that God has given them permission to oppress women. Jesus came to change the way we think about God. In response, abuse is rebuked and thoroughly condemned by God and will not be accepted in His presence on Judgment Day. Throughout the New Testament scriptures, we see that Jesus did not allow people to be physically harmed in His presence. In John 8:3-12, we see that a woman was caught in the act of adultery and that, according to the civil laws taken from the Mosaic laws, she was supposed to be stoned. However, Jesus had other plans:

> "Then the scribes and Pharisees brought to Him a woman caught in adultery. And when they had set her in the midst, they said to Him, 'Teacher, this woman was caught in adultery, in the very act. Now Moses, in the law, commanded us that such should be stoned. But what do You say?' This they said, testing Him, that they might have something of which to accuse Him. But Jesus stooped down and wrote on the ground with His finger, as though He did not hear. So, when they continued asking Him, He raised Himself up and said to them, 'He who is without sin among you, let him throw a stone at her first.' And again He stooped down and wrote on the ground. Then those who heard it, being convicted by their conscience, went out one by one, beginning with the oldest even to the last. And Jesus was left alone, and the woman standing in the midst. When Jesus had raised Himself up and saw no one but the woman, He said to her, 'Woman, where are

> *those accusers of yours? Has no one condemned*
> *you?' She said, 'No one, Lord.' And Jesus said to*
> *her, 'Neither do I condemn you; go and sin no*
> *more.' Then Jesus spoke to them again, saying, 'I*
> *am the light of the world. He who follows Me*
> *shall not walk in darkness, but have the light of*
> *life.'"*

This story reflects God being viewed with a new perception. When Jesus refused to stone the lady who was guilty of breaking one of God's previous commandments, He went against the current perception of God at that time. So, right away, based on the former perception of God, Jesus was considered to be wrong for what He did. This is just one story out of many that show how Jesus was establishing a new perception of God.

Then, after Christ's death and resurrection, we see in the story of Paul's conversion how Jesus still felt about His people being abused. Saul was a Jew also known as Paul (which was his Greek name). He was a valiant and very passionate follower of the instructions of Abraham and the Mosaic laws. Saul was one who joyfully stoned people who followed the new perception of God that had been sent through His Son, Jesus Christ. Christ's followers all steered clear of Paul because getting too close to him and being discovered to be a follower of Christ meant they would be regarded as blasphemers and betrayers of the former perception of God. They would be stoned because of it. Well, in Acts 9:3-5, while Saul was traveling on the road of Damascus, Jesus called him out and rebuked him for persecuting His people:

> *"Now as he went on his way, he approached Damascus, and suddenly a light from heaven shone around him. And falling to the ground, he heard a voice saying to him, 'Saul, Saul, why are you persecuting me?' And he said, 'Who are you, Lord?' And he said, 'I am Jesus, whom you are persecuting.'"*

As we can see again, regardless of whether a person is male or female, Jesus is not okay with His people being oppressed or abused. To stone, oppress, or abuse one of Christ's followers is to cause Jesus to share in the hurt and pain of those vile actions. In the world today, we may not use physical stones, but when a person is the victim of domestic abuse, it feels like verbal, emotional, and sometimes physical stones are being thrown at them every day. To use the name of Jesus Christ to physically harm, stone, or abuse anyone (regardless of belief or faith) for any reason is completely unacceptable. God does not hate people, nor does He desire to oppress people. The only ideal that God hates and desires to oppress and kill is the root of sinful behaviors that destroy our relationship with Him and one another. Today, the perception of God sent through Christ is the only perception that His true followers are to embrace and follow. God's entire reason for sending His Son was to restore humanity's relationship with Him and to redefine His perception of love as a new foundation for the intimate relationships between men and women and for all relationships among humanity that God deems acceptable.

CHAPTER 7

THE GREAT OPPRESSION

Sadly, as a woman growing up in the Christian church, I experienced sexism, religious abuse, and female oppression all at the hands of men who were blinded by the curse of Eve. Abusive behaviors from many men within the public forum of the Christian church are just as normal as abusive behaviors from men outside the church. As a matter of fact, I was raised in a home with emotional and verbal domestic abuse, and the acceptable male-dominant behavior was hailed as God's truth in our home. Throughout my years as a child and a teenager, I noticed how my stepfather illegally used his gender to oppress my mother. He knew my mother had a call on her life to minister and preach in the public forum of the Christian church. However, my stepfather followed blind doctrines. Under the mindset of the curse of Eve, he fought my mother every chance he got, rebuking her, trying to forbid her from preaching, arguing with her, demeaning her, disrespecting her, and treating her like a second-class citizen in her own home. So, not only did my mother receive opposition from my stepdad, but, based on the majority of Christian doctrines and beliefs, her call to preach within the public forum of the Christian church was rejected as well. I'm not saying my mother was innocent and never did anything wrong to my stepfather, but there is never an excuse for a human being to be habitually mistreated and disrespected simply because of his or her sex. Sadly, the chauvinistic attitude that comes with thinking under the curse of Eve ruled our home while I was growing up. Eventually, the male-dominated and chauvinistic behavior drove my mother into a state of deep depression, breaking her down mentally and emotionally in her later years. My stepdad was so partial to males that he even treated me— an innocent child—like I was nothing more than a confused, stupid, second-class human being, just because I was female. So, in our home, the mindset of the curse of Eve reigned supreme. In my life, it really should not have surprised me that I went out and found a familiar atmosphere of abuse and married into it. During my marriage, my mind was not doing its best when it came to my perception of men. My stepfather had violated me when I was young, then a second time when I was an adult in my 30s, a few years before I married. He violated me twice without remorse or repentance, all while holding a Bible in his hands. As a matter of fact, after I exposed the first violation, I felt anger from him for years. After that second violation, I became hurt and angry. I stepped out of the mind of Christ; I lost the sense of value for my self- respect and virginity that I had been raised to maintain. Sadly, before I married, I went out in anger and confusion and lost my virginity to a guy who really did not value me or the gift that I gave him. So, there I was, feeling the pain of having been born a woman, bound to look for a man to rule over me and make me feel loved…yet instead of love I found the remnants of the curse alive and well in my own mind, causing me to live out my life under the perception of the curse of Eve.

The Bias Perception

For centuries, a large majority of the Christian church has used the Bible under the thoughts and perception of the curse of Eve to oppress women, over-exalt men, and teach that God forbids women from leading or pastoring men within the public forum of the church. Although the acceptance of female leaders within the Christian church seems to have progressed to the point that many women are being celebrated as senior pastors, many men within the Christian church still do not accept this idea. Some Christian men are still blinded by the curse of Eve and are under the impression that God created their sex to be superior to women. Sadly, some men still think that God left them on earth to rule over women and to set women straight by heavily monitoring what women can and cannot do. In an effort to continue oppressing women, many men within the Christian church have created platforms for their wives or other women within the church to minister solely through women's ministries. Unfortunately, according to what God has revealed to me about this issue, many of the men who appear to accept women are okay with females taking a role in ministry as long as they are leading other women. Sadly, many Christian men still have hearts that oppose women pastoring men in senior-level positions within the Christian church. So, apparently, some men appear to simply be embracing equality by accepting women as a source of secondary income for their organizations. However, I believe that God sees their hearts and that, to Him, their acceptance of women is nothing more than an illusion. Unfortunately, the blindness within a vast majority of the Christian church in this area is so pronounced that the biases selection of keynote speakers for women's and men's conferences is so evident. For example, a well-known pastor of a mega-organization in Texas holds massive conferences for men and women every year. Well, after conducting some research on the people invited to speak at his conferences, I noticed that, during the past few years, the women's conferences have included female keynote speakers but also at least two or more men, including the pastor himself. However, for the past few years, the pastor has booked only male keynote speakers for the men's conferences, with no female speakers included at all. To some, this may not be a big deal. However, based on what I am discovering, to God, something is seriously wrong with how many men and women think within the Christian church. The curse of Eve has distorted the perception of how a man sees a woman and vice versa. I mean, how outright biased is it to say that it's okay for men to minister to and influence women at women's conferences, but it's not okay for women to influence and minister to men at men's conferences? I wonder how it's okay for a woman to carry a male child for nine months, give birth to the child, be a major influence in his life (and perhaps raise the male child by herself), and then, all of a sudden, not be allowed to minister to males within the public forum of the church. It is apparent that within the Christian church, a man can outgrow the influence of a woman, but a woman can't outgrow a man's influence. Basically, women "need" to be ministered to by men, but they don't "need" women to minister to them.

On the one hand, I think that maybe the pastor is not aware of what he is doing. Then, on the other hand, I think,

'How can he not be aware,' because the bias seems so evident to me. What is the real reason why this pastor and so many others feel that they can prevent women from ministering at men's conferences, but place themselves at women's conferences? The gender-biased selection of keynote speakers for men's and women's conferences is a great example of the evident, biased perception that I notice is so prevalent in most of the overall public forum of the Christian church. Some of us might think, 'Well, maybe the fellas just need a break from women for a weekend, or perhaps it's better for men to minister to men because a man knows what to say to another man.' However, if that were the case, women should be the only ones ministering to women...but yet, some men always seem to find their way onto the roster for a women's conference. In reality, it is apparent to the heart of God, through Christ perception, that this behavior on the part of certain leaders within the Christian church is unacceptable. As a woman, I am not fighting to speak—nor am I really interested in speaking—at men's conferences.

Just for the record, that's too much testosterone in one building for me. I would rather be at home binge-watching a TV show on Netflix or Amazon Prime or having a lady's day at a spa, but that is just my personal preference. I'm not saying the men's conference is bad; I just believe in giving the fellas space if and when they need it. However, my personal opinion does not change my overall point. I am addressing the apparent perception that is rooted in the curse of Eve, which creates the biased expectations of males and females within a large majority of the public forum of the Christian church. The sad thing is, when women like me speak up against the hypocrisy and biased perceptions within the Christian church, we are harshly rebuked and looked upon as rebellious. We are called "Jezebels" or any other Biblical name that is usually mentioned in ignorance, with absolutely no understanding of why women like me say what we say. When those men judge, they do so blindly and harshly, without God's heart of empathy and lacking compassion toward the issues being addressed. Sadly, people still have not gotten the memo that the biblical image of Jezebel has nothing to do with her gender; rather, her controlling behavior is what defines her. Jezebel's controlling behavior is found in men the same as it is found in women. Considering how many men have fallen prey to the blinders of the curse of Eve and exalted themselves as being equal to God, setting themselves above women while holding the very reins of our lives like we are dog's on leashes, who sounds like the "Jezebel" to you? Women who talk like I do, trying to expose and sincerely correct an evident issue? Or the men blinded by the curse, who are actually the ones holding the leash?

The Blindness of Men

Let me start this section by revealing the error in what many men believe. I will do this by detailing the scriptures in the New Testament that is taught within the public forum of the Christian church and that is used to justify its oppression of women. These verses are used by many men who have been blinded by the curse of Eve and who consequently oppress women within the Christian church, forbidding them from pastoring and leading men in the public forum of the church. Let's start with the verses recorded in the Book of 1 Timothy 2:11-15:

> *"Let a woman learn in silence with all submission. And I do not permit a woman to teach or to have authority over a man, but to be in silence. For Adam was formed first, then Eve. And Adam was not deceived, but the woman being deceived, fell into transgression. Nevertheless, she will be saved in childbearing if they continue in faith, love, and holiness, with self-control."*

Okay, here we see that this verse is perceived as silencing women in the public forum of the church. Due to a lack of understanding of God's character and heart toward His original order for both males and females, many male leaders within the public forum of the Christian church see women from the perception of the curse of Eve. Many men today emulate the way this verse was perceived back then; they aim to silence women in the public forum of the Christian Church. So, basically, this verse is perceived in a manner contrary to the order of equality that God originally gave to both males and females.

In my opinion, the perception issue is so evident because, in verse 12, the writer states, *"I do not permit a woman to teach."* The writer did not say that God or Jesus commanded that. The passage of scripture that I am using is taken from the New King James Version. However, if you read other versions of the Bible, you will see that the writer addresses the wife and not just women in general. However, regardless of the version that is read, the writer also refers to Eve as being the sole transgressor, the only one who was deceived into disobeying God. Because of that, the writer states, it's her fault that Adam ate of the forbidden fruit. Therefore, a woman should never lead a man. As a punishment, she is forbidden from speaking to men or leading them in the public forum of the church. The writer goes on to state that the woman will be spared from the curse of pain during childbearing if she continues on in the faith. Based on my personal study of the authorship of Timothy, I believe the author is unknown. A few sources say that Paul was the author, but more sources say that he was not. There is no proof, either way, to determine exactly what happened. However, what is apparent is that, in hindsight, the verses do not detail the full curse of Eve being broken. The way the writer addresses women here, it seems as if Jesus' death and resurrection destroyed only the childbearing curse and not the entire curse that removed the model in which the man rules over the woman. I am not sure who wrote this or what exactly happened, but it is very clear to me that today this verse is not perceived through the eyes of Christ. Based on how the verses appear to address women during that time in a partial sense, maybe the writer struggled with the same veils of the curse of Eve that we struggle with today.

Our next set of passages is from 1 Corinthians 11:1-16 and 1 Corinthians 14:34-35. These are verses that are also used to oppress women in the Christian church:

> *"Imitate me, just as I also imitate Christ. Now I praise you, brethren, that you remember me in all things and keep the traditions just as I delivered them to you. But I want you to know that the head of every man is Christ, the head of woman is man, and the head of Christ is God. Every man praying or prophesying, having his head covered, dishonors his head. But every woman who prays*

or prophesies with her head uncovered dishonors her head, for that is one and the same as if her head were shaved. For if a woman is not covered, let her also be shorn. But if it is shameful for a woman to be shorn or shaved, let her be covered. For a man indeed ought not to cover his head, since he is the image and glory of God; but woman is the glory of man. For man is not from woman, but woman from man. Nor was man created for the woman, but woman for the man. For this reason, the woman ought to have a symbol of authority on her head, because of the angels. Nevertheless, neither is man independent of woman, nor woman independent of man, in the Lord. For as woman came from man, even so man also comes through woman; but all things are from God. Judge among yourselves. Is it proper for a woman to pray to God with her head uncovered? Does not even nature itself teach you that if a man has long hair, it is a dishonor to him? But if a woman has long hair, it is a glory to her; for her hair is given to her for a covering. But if anyone seems to be contentious, we have no such custom, nor do the churches of God."

Finally, the other popular verses that are so widely used to oppress women pastoring at a senior level within the Christian church are 1 Corinthians 14:34-35:

> *"Let your women keep silent in the churches, for they are not permitted to speak; but they are to be submissive, as the law also says. And if they want to learn something, let them ask their own husbands at home; for it is shameful for women to speak in church."*

We must understand that 1 Corinthians 11:1-16 was talking about the customs of that time, as we know that the whole concept of the superior male and inferior female came in under the curse of Eve. As I researched what was going on during the time when 1 Corinthians 14:34-35 was written, I discovered that women were disrespecting the speaker by blurting out information during meetings. The speaker corrected the situation by using the guidelines of Jewish customs, which reflected the Mosaic Laws.

After taking time to study the authorship of 1 Corinthians, I discovered that it is speculated that either Paul wrote it alone, it was a collaborative work, or someone else wrote it. Truthfully, the Bible was written so long ago that unless an author left their name on a writing, we will never really know who wrote what. As I said before, regardless of who wrote the passages in 1 Corinthians or 1 Timothy, the verses are not perceived correctly today. After reading those verses, I would say that, again, they are misinterpreted because of the roots of the curse of Eve that veils our minds from seeing God's original order.

All the passages of scripture that I have shared are the most common verses used today to argue that a woman must have a man over her in regard to leading men in public worship within the public forum of the Christian church. Whoever wrote 1 Corinthians 11:1 stated that he was imitating Christ...but was he really imitating Christ? I don't recall Christ promoting Jewish customs over having a heart-to-heart relationship with God. As a matter of fact, as you read the Bible, you'll find that Jesus constantly challenged many of the civil laws and Jewish customs during His time (as I shared in Chapter 6 from John 8:1-12). Throughout the life of Christ, I do not recall reading that Jesus implemented or enforced the covering of heads among those who followed Him. I'm not saying that those who followed Him did not wear head coverings due to the customs of their time, but I don't recall Jesus enforcing Jewish traditions among His disciples as much as the writer of this passage of scripture did. Based on these verses, it appears that the writer's perception of Christ was formed solely through the eyes of the former Jewish customs regarding how to treat women. What's funny about men who follow and teach 1 Corinthians 11:14 today is how picky and choosy some men can be about what they say they believe. For instance, today, for those who follow and misperceive these verses, a man's hair can be longer in length and be excused, without correction. However, if a woman stands up to become a senior pastor of a church, some men will use these verses to judge her with harsh rebukes. Technically, because Christ is the head of His church, God did not ever establish the male gender as the one to take dominion or rule over a woman in the public forum of the church, or anywhere else for that matter. The reality is, if a woman is subjugated by the male gender in public worship, this would literally reflect the illusion that God created the male to rule over the female. Once God's heart is seen through Christ perception, it becomes evident that the image of male dominance that many people see and perceive in these verses today does not reflect God's original order at all.

In the verses we read in 1 Corinthians 14:34-35, the writer referred to the "law" of God as being his source. What law was the writer referring to? Before I answer that question, we must understand that all the Apostles' writings in the New Testament were intended to build the structure of the early church. First, we must realize that any letter Paul or anyone else wrote to the churches was sent to correct specific situations in the cities where Christians lived during that time. Everything Paul and the other writers wrote was intended to guide the early church in living orderly lives in their relationships with God and one another. Then he refers to the law of God as his source, but here is the deal: The law to which he referred was not the laws that Jesus left. After researching those verses, I found that the word "Nomos" is the Greek word for "law." Nomos is defined as "anything established, anything received by usage, a custom, wage, law: a command, a different law from that which God has given, of the Mosaic law, etc." So, as you can see, whoever wrote these passages literally perceived men as being superior to women. It is very evident that the writer was still blinded by the curse of Eve and still treated women according to the order that had been written in the Mosaic laws. As I stated before, the Old Testament was written from the perception and mindset of the curses of Adam and Eve. Everything within those laws was about man performing outward deeds to please God. However, if you read through the laws, you'll find that they never promised that the deeds would change the hearts of those who obeyed. Every deed was performed to obtain favor, salvation, and blessings from God. Yet when Jesus showed up, He focused on the heart and made it clear that only a relationship with Him could connect a person to God's heart and restore God's original order for relationships within a person's life.

Regardless of who wrote what and why, not one verse in the entire Bible that I have read liberated the woman or man by fully acknowledging that Jesus broke the curse of Eve. So, the perception held by many men today can simply be due to a lack of information or maybe the man's inability to think and see beyond the veiled perception of the curse of Eve. Whoever wrote the passages in 1 Corinthians could assign a woman's role in public worship based only on the pattern given in the former laws because those laws were all they had to go on. Those laws were still an active part of society during that time. Another thing to take note of, is that the early church did not have a Bible with as many books of the New Testament as we do today. Some of those who walked with Jesus knew what to do by personal experience and by actually being there to hear Jesus' instructions. However, their generation expired, and a new breed of followers was led only by the Holy Spirit, without a fully written New Testament to give them instructions. Sadly, throughout the New Testament, fruitless works from the former covenant were constantly being rebuked and corrected by Paul, who was given proper credit for writing the most books in the Bible. Truthfully, the only written words back then were the fully written Old Testament books and the individual letters that were actively being written during that time to complete the New Testament books. So, Paul and all of the Apostles back then did not have another model upon which to build the New Covenant church and to show that the curses of Adam and Eve were truly broken. Considering, Jewish customs from the former order were a major part of life for the New Covenant converts, the early church truly had no idea how to build a New Covenant church based on the essence of a new perception of God sent through Jesus Christ. I don't believe that those in the New Covenant church oppressed women on purpose; the former order was simply all they knew. However, today we do know better. We have a lot more information about Jesus than any other generation in human history. Yet most of the Christian church still chooses to put the curse of Eve on full display by denying the liberating evidence of God's heart sent through Jesus Christ, which is intended to make women equal leaders in the public forum of the Christian church and the home.

Based on the foundations that Jesus left and the situational truths that other writers established, there is a big difference in the perception toward women throughout the entire Bible. For those who believe that Paul did write the passages in 1 Corinthians, we must take a moment to understand who Paul was and where he came from. Before Jesus called Paul to be an Apostle, he was a valiant and very passionate follower of the Mosaic laws, to the point that he killed many Christians from the early church as a means of honoring those former laws. So, basically, the only example of a system set in place to worship God came from the Old Order. In reality, the Old Order not only banned women, but also banned gentiles (i.e., males and females of non-Jewish blood) from ministering to God as priests in the temple. Of course, Paul or whoever wrote those passages did not oppress women on purpose. I'm sure the writer of those passages gave instructions believing that he was doing God a service; he thought that was what God wanted him to do. Paul or whoever wrote those passages did the best he could to build Christ's church with one ear to heaven and one ear to what was familiar to him during that time. Those who wrote those passages were no different from many of the leaders today. In a sense, we are all fragile souls who simply want to be loved and accepted by God, and we are willing to do whatever we think He wants so that we can gain His love and acceptance. Even those today who misperceive these verses believe they are literally doing God a service by ruling over a woman and keeping a woman in a place of oppression.

The Great Error

Regardless of whether Paul or someone else wrote these passages, it is evident that whoever wrote them was definitely perceiving women according to God's former orders. The former laws of Moses were written through the perception of Adam and Eve. Those perceptions are cursed. When Christians think according to these cursed perceptions, they cause many within the Christian church to inadvertently miss out on the love, respect, and equality that pours from the heart of God toward both women and men. In my life, the curse of Eve has definitely influenced my thinking. Just like it was with the writers of those passages, the curse of Eve is embedded in the thoughts of both men and women. Only when we submit to God's Holy Spirit by believing in the death and resurrection of Jesus Christ will we see the end of the inferior and superior thought patterns that destroy male and female relationships. As I mentioned earlier, how can the writer of 1 Timothy acknowledge that Jesus broke the curse of pain in childbearing and yet disregard the destruction of the curse of the gender of man ruling over and dominating the woman? Sorry, but once a person truly sees the loving heart of God through Christ perception, it is impossible to accept only a partial truth. The former perception goes against the New Order that God sent through Jesus Christ. The very loud foundational message of Jesus Christ is superior to that of Paul and every other writer in both the New and Old Testaments. Jesus was not a situational minister. He spoke words to build the foundation for His followers. Jesus was the divine Son of God sent to build a bridge for all humanity to approach God and have a relationship with God and one another. Whoever wrote 1 Timothy disregarded the full curse being broken off Eve. By disregarding the fact that the curse had been broken off Eve, the writer also disregarded the curse that had been broken off Adam as well. Since, man is connected to woman, both sexes have suffered drastically because of this. It is truly and absolutely impossible to liberate the woman without liberating the man. In regard to the verses we discussed, after some research on all the verses I have mentioned so far, I don't believe that the verses we have covered were ever intended to instruct the foundation of Christians today. Technically, during the time when they were written, those verses were tainted with the wrong perception of what Christ really desired for women. Truthfully, the Apostles were leaders in a growing and developing new church being formed, so the books written by the Apostles were writings that were captured at that time.

I have found any perception captured by a human being can change. So since the Apostles were mere human men who were used by God, their perception of God had to grow and evolve into the mind of Christ, just like anyone of us today. So in hindsight the new Covenant perception of God's order within relationships was actually dismissed by men after Christ death and resurrection. Sadly, due to a lack of information about the further development of the early church, those of us today will never really know if the perception of the Apostles back then ever discovered God's original order for women and men in relationships and in the public forum of the Christian church. As a writer I have reviewed my previous writings and seen where my thoughts, beliefs, and perceptions about God and relationships has changed from where they once were. I also realize the only person in the Bible whose character, order, and perception will never change is God's. Unlike how mortal men and women change our perception, God's order sent through Jesus Christ will never change. I also want to say that if Paul did write the passages in 1 Corinthians, I still acknowledge and honor him as a bold Apostle who deserves respect. I understand his perception and why he said what he said based on the situation at that time. However, I also believe that in spite of the evident lack of liberty conveyed to women through the passages in 1 Corinthians and 1 Timothy, overall, the goal of each New Testament writer was to point to Christ—and not themselves—as the foundation and cornerstone of the New Covenant Church. I am sure that if Paul did write those passages in 1 Corinthians and 1 Timothy, and if he had been aware that those who confess Christ today would be following the instructions, he gave during that time more than they are following the foundation of truth and liberated love sent through Jesus Christ, he would definitely not be happy. Today, I am quite sure he would sternly rebuke the majority of the Christian church (1 Corinthians 3:4-11).

Jesus Liberated Women

Throughout the gospels, a person can clearly see that Jesus embraced women by inviting them in. Jesus surrounded himself with women; a woman prepared Jesus for His burial. Mary Magdalene was the first person who saw Jesus in His risen form and who recognized Him. He commanded her to go and tell His disciples that He had risen. I would say that Mary was the first apostle called by Christ Himself. All apostles are called personally by Christ and not by mortal men. The first thing Jesus did when He rose from the grave was to send a woman to talk to his male disciples and give them His message and declare His resurrection. Then, after the ascension of Christ, He authorized 120 to go into the upper room. Included in that upper room were both males and females—Jesus' mother and family were there as well (Acts 1:12-14). Truthfully, the only stories that we know about in the New Testament are housed in the 27 books to which we have access within the canonized Bible. Other than the lost books of the Bible that have surfaced, we do not know everything that was ever written and inspired by God. We must also remember that because 120 people were in the upper room, the acts of the apostles during that time were so great, I doubt we would be able to read all their stories in one lifetime. During those days, large numbers were being added to the body of Christ—3,000 members at one time. So, as believers in Christ, we must not allow what we can see and read in the Bible to prevent us from realizing that the acts of both males and females in the New Testament were much more than we will ever know.

The Sacraments

Sadly, in addition to all that we went over, many men within the Christian church today have created more reasons why women can't lead in the public forum of the church. Many men who are still blinded by the curse of Eve believe that a woman should not serve in sacraments. This translates into serving communion, performing water baptisms, and any other service that men within the Christian church regard as a sacrament. Many men within the Christian church establish their own rules to oppress women and dictate what a woman can and cannot do. They do this innocently, thinking that they are doing God a service, all while disregarding the fullness of what Jesus has done. Instead of embracing Christ by acknowledging that the curse has been broken, they follow the same pattern of those who wrote the verses in 1 Timothy and 1 Corinthians using God's old laws regarding women in public worship. I find it interesting that Paul was the one who also said that our bodies are the temple of the Lord (1 Corinthians 3:16, 6:19). Then, in Revelation 1:6, we see that Christ made us priests. Some translations say Christ made us kings ("kings" is inclusive of "queens") and priests. However, again, to those blinded by the curse of Eve, apparently a woman is excluded from those liberties. Hebrews 4:16 reads:

> *"Let us therefore come boldly to the throne of grace, that we may obtain mercy and find grace to help in time of need."*

Now, here we are as women with Christ's instructions, declaring that both the male and female bodies are God's Holy Temples. Then males and females are counted equally as priests and, finally, males and females are equally able to boldly go before God and receive mercy and grace. On the other hand, we are being told by many mortal men within the public forum of the Christian church that God did not ordain women to pastor or serve sacraments. What I find interesting is that throughout history, women have ruled entire countries. As a matter of fact, Queen Mary I, Lady Jane Grey, and Queen Elizabeth I, among many other female queens, ruled over England and other providences during the time when the Catholic Church ruled with the Bible. However, within the public forum of the dominant Catholic and Protestant Churches back then, women were banned from leading. So, basically, when the Catholic Church reigned in complete control during the Dark Ages, women were ruling the very country in which the church operated...and yet women were oppressed and not allowed to have authority in the isolated public forum of the Catholic Church. In hindsight, to those associated with the Christian church, God is okay with a woman being the queen of a nation, but He is not okay with a woman being in a leadership position in an isolated building that people call a church. I don't think so; something sounds fishy to me. What both men and women have been taught throughout a large majority of the Christian church is perceived through the eyes of the curse of Eve and not through the eyes of Jesus Christ.

CHAPTER 8

PROJECTED BELIEFS

When I started writing this book, it was like therapy. After making the hard decision to remove myself from an abusive situation and to divorce my husband, I was frustrated and irritated. Honestly, for some reason, I was disappointed in the Christian church. I felt as if everything I had been taught about marriage had not helped me in my marriage at all. I had been learning about biblical marriage throughout my teen and adult life. As a single woman, I joyfully attended meetings that taught about the marriage relationship—and yet my marriage failed because of the actual perception that those teachings had conveyed to me and my husband. Unfortunately, the distorted perception of God that those teachings conveyed only made my marriage worse and much more abusive. All I really wanted was to be a team and work together, joined as one like God created in the beginning and like Jesus encouraged.

However, as you read, you will find that the predominant relationship model within the Christian church is not taught according to God's original order.

A Literal Disaster

As I mentioned at the beginning of this book, the Bible is the most misquoted, misinterpreted, misused, and manipulated book in human history. People have used the Bible to justify both sex-based and race-based divisions. The very divisive perception of God's standards for both the female and male sexes in a relationship has impacted relationships both inside and outside the Christian church. Within the Christian church, one of the most widely used and popular verses for teaching on the subject of marriage is found in Ephesians 5:22-25, 33:

> *"Wives, submit to your own husbands, as to the Lord. For the husband is head of the wife, as also Christ is head of the church; and He is the Savior of the body. Therefore, just as the church is subject to Christ, so let the wives be to their own husbands in everything. Husbands, love your*

wives, just as Christ also loved the church and gave Himself for her, Nevertheless, let each one of you in particular so love his own wife as himself, and let the wife see that she respects her husband."

Technically, these verses can be perceived in one of two ways. One way is that they are symbolic, comparing a man's level of love to Christ's level of love. Basically, according to this perception, a man is encouraged to be selfless and simply love and cherish his wife. Then the woman is innocently encouraged to respect the husband's efforts to love her sacrificially, like Jesus Christ loves His church. The verses can be perceived as though Jesus was providing a simple example of the measure of selfless, respectful, and sacrificial love that should be present in a relationship between the man and the woman. The other way these verses can be perceived is literal: declaring that God has exalted the man as being superior to the woman. Based on statistics that prove there are far more women—both inside and outside the Christian church—who are abused, oppressed, harassed, and bullied by men, it is evident that most people interpret and perceive these verses literally. We can clearly see that the way in which these verses are read paints a picture that literally establishes the male sex as superior to the female sex by placing the male sex on the same level as Christ and also by giving the male the full responsibility of loving the woman at a level equal to God.

When taken literally, these verses clearly place the male gender in a superior state to rule over the woman at the same level that Christ rules over His church. After hearing sermon after sermon and teaching after teaching about these verses, one discovers that the man is the only one taught to love (not respect) his wife, while the woman is the only one taught to submit to and respect (not love) her husband. It all sounds nice and innocent, but the misinterpretation of these verses has literally encouraged men to abandon respect for women and disregard the foundational standards of simple love, respect, and mutual submission toward women that God originally ordained. The literal interpretation of these verses has been, and still is, deadly for women. As a matter of fact, while writing this book, I heard a story about a Christian woman who was in an abusive domestic marriage and whose husband murdered her...and, yes, they were both involved with the Christian church. Sadly, more than likely, their relationship was structured based on the literal perception of these teachings. Now, truthfully, I don't know for sure whether the woman I mentioned was taught the literal perception of these verses. However, almost everyone who is a part of the Christian church has been taught these standards as the superior model for the marriage relationship.

The Illusion of Truth

What I have noticed about the teachings within the Christian church is that most of the doctrines that are used to give instructions for the marriage relationship are never based on God's original order for relationships. Instead, within the Christian church, the verses in Ephesians that were written to the Church of Ephesus reign superior to the foundational message that God sent Jesus Christ to implement. After doing some research on the Book of Ephesians, I discovered that some say Paul is the author of Ephesians, while others say he is not. Today, most Christians are taught that Paul was the original author. Again, regardless of who wrote these passages, the way in which they are perceived today is not in line with God's original order before the fall. It appears that even the verses themselves are still reflective of the curse of Eve; they still encourage male pre-eminence and dominance. I'm not sure what exactly happened, but I am sure that these verses were written according to the pattern of God's former order to correct a specific situation during that time. They were not intended to serve as the overall order for all relationships among Christians.

Sadly, within a large majority of the Christian church today, as long as a man simply attends Sunday morning services and faithfully gives monetary gifts, he is deemed the head of his household and his bad behavior is often overlooked. Basically, as long as the fallen image of man is predominant, a man can be prideful, hard-hearted, insecure, narcissistic, and abusive. Yet, because he was born a man, he is protected by God and placed on the same level as Christ, as being the covering and head of the woman. Some Christian men embrace the concept that because Christ is present in their lives, it is through Him that they become the symbol of Christ, set in a superior position by God to cover the woman like Christ covers His church. The Christian men who think this way are innocently misperceiving the concept of salvation through Jesus Christ. The truth is, even though some Christian men may truly be born again, this does not mean that their sex is equal to God and placed by God to rule over women. God and His character and heart, sent through Jesus Christ, reign superior to both men and women. God gave His only Son Jesus Christ the passage to project His heart and character through the lives of both men and women. So, even when a Christian man is sincerely loving his wife, it is not the man, but the superior love of Christ, that pours through him. Because both the Christian man and the Christian woman have the capacity to love like Christ, they are both called to walk joined together as one, covered by God's love for them and by their love for one another. It is the love of God that pours through the man to the woman and vice versa. So, in reality, due to the fall of Adam and Eve, neither the man nor the woman can take credit for showing a love that is not truly reflective of their fallen nature. Therefore, a mortal man can never be placed by God to rule over a woman on God's level. That same fact applies to women; a woman cannot be placed by God to rule over a man. If Christ is removed from the equation, neither a mortal man nor a mortal woman has the capacity to love according to God's original order. Yet when the heart of God is seen through Jesus Christ, His loving order is clearly conveyed through the hearts of the men and women who believe in His love. So, the call to love, respect, and walk in mutual submission should be reflected by both the male and the female. However, as we have learned so far, God's original order for relationships is far from what is taught and believed throughout a vast majority of the Christian church.

The Situational Concept of Christian Marriage

Today, the basis for every marriage conference, marriage counseling session, relationship event, and Sunday morning sermon about marriage is the Biblical instructions based on Ephesians 5:22-25, 33. You may be asking, "Are there other verses that the Christian church uses to teach about marriage?" Yes, there are; 1 Peter 3:1-7 and Colossians 3:18-19, they all basically say the same thing. However, I have found that the verses that are detailed and discussed the most are those in the Book of Ephesians 5:22-25, 33. If you read 1 Peter 3:1-7 and Colossians 3:18-19, you will find that all the verses I mentioned are perceived by many within the Christian church today under the same curse of Eve that is also perceived in Ephesians 5:22-25, 33.

Although, these verses seem harmless, when they fall into the hands of an already prideful, hard-hearted, insecure, narcissistic, and abusive man, they become deadly to a woman. Now, in any case, regardless of who wrote the verses in question, I do not believe that the writer ever intended for these verses to be taught as superior to the foundation for all relationships that God originally established and restored through Jesus Christ. However, most Christian doctrines present these verses in Ephesians as God's highest order, as if God established it. Unlike the writers of the New Testament letters, the standards that God sent Jesus to establish were not based on circumstances or isolated situations; they were based on the eternal foundation of God's loving order for the male and female relationship. Because love and respect go together, the totality of love will always encompass respect. Most teachings about marriage within the Christian church are, sadly, not built on the liberating message of love sent through Jesus Christ. They always seem to separate love from respect. Most teachings in the Christian church use the name

of Jesus and mention love, but God's heart and loving character for unity between the genders (and even among the rac-
es) is seen only vaguely, through the veils of Eve's curse. Sadly, when it comes to the marriage relationship, these are the
main verses used by the majority of the Christian Church.
They are also the same verses that many men use to justify
abusing their wives. Just to show you how blinded by Eve's
curse some of the study material is within the Christian
church, I researched chapter 5 of Ephesians and discovered a
commentary that also taught that God perceives women as
being inferior to men. According to Matthew Henry's Commentary on the Whole Bible,

*The apostle assigns the reason of this submission from wives: For
the husband is the head of the wife. The metaphor is taken from the head
in the natural body, which, being the seat of reason, of wisdom, and of
knowledge, and the fountain of sense and motion, is more excellent than
the rest of the body. God has given the man the pre-eminence and a right
to direct and govern by creation, and in that original law of the relation,
Thy desire shall be to thy husband, and he shall rule over thee. Whatever
there is of uneasiness in this, it is an effect of sin coming into the world.
Generally, too, the man has (what he ought to have) a superiority in
wisdom and knowledge. He is therefore the head, even as Christ is the
head of the church.*

So, as you can see, many men within the Christian
church have been taught to literally perceive themselves as

superior and as having more knowledge and wisdom than women do. That passage referred to the curse of Eve as being a relevant mindset celebrated by God. In addition to what most Christian men have been taught, most Christian women have been taught that they are inferior and of lesser value than men, that they are not as wise or knowledgeable. So, within a majority of the Christian church, both males and females have been building their marriages and general relationships through the perception of the curse of Eve and not through the liberating perception of God's heart, which is seen only through the perception of Jesus Christ. As we know, we cannot have the perception of Christ if we do not think and believe in the revelation of the order and character of God that Jesus Christ represented.

My Collision with Mr. Literal

I was raised to follow the model for marriage written in Ephesians. As a matter of fact, my ex-husband used those verses to abuse me. He would literally say, "The Bible does not command the man to respect his wife, but it commands the woman to respect her husband. So, you are supposed to respect me, and I don't have to respect you because that is not what the Bible instructs a man to do." He used those same verses to explain why, as a man, he did not have to answer to me for anything. He believed, based on these verses, that I had to submit to him and do what he said. Because the Bible said so, he was exempt from mutual submission. Therefore, according to him, he was also exempt from discussing pertinent information that affected our relationship. For example, we got a credit card in both of our names and although we paid it off quickly, I needed to see the credit card so I could add the information to my list of cards but he refused to let me see the card. Because I was the woman, I had to answer to him for everything. No matter what I said, because I was the wife, he did not have to listen to or even consider what I said. He had to be the one who made the final decision without my involvement. Well, after almost two years of being abused by a man who held the Bible in his hands, I realized something was very wrong, not only with how my ex-husband perceived these verses but how I had been raised to perceive these verses. My ex-husband would disrespect me by constantly screaming and yelling at me with no apology.

He would gaslight me and control how long I spent with my family. He tried to isolate me and instill fear in me. For the first six months, I allowed him to control, manipulate, and intimidate me. I let him dictate what he wanted, and I never spoke up. Due to what I learned about relationships in the Christian church, I allowed him to control and disrespect me as if that were what God approved of. Due to my sincere desire to please God based on the literal meaning of these verses I had been taught, I sought to submit to and respect my husband, to truly try hard to please him, as most women raised in the Christian church do. He was from a country in Africa that looked down on African Americans, and, unfortunately, I allowed him to habitually demean my heritage as well. He looked at me as his enemy and disparaged me at every turn. No matter what I did to show him that we had to be a team, he made it his mission to intimidate me with his yelling and to destroy my self-esteem with his words. It was so bad that when we were together in public when it was time to leave our location, he would beckon me to come like I were a dog on a leash. His behavior toward me was disgraceful and insolent.

Thankfully, before I married, I had a really healthy and blossoming relationship with God through Jesus Christ. My relationship with God always consisted of communication between Him and I. However, just because God is always talking does not mean I was or am always listening. Sadly, considering the fact that I voluntarily jumped into a marriage with an abuser, I would say that, at that time, I turned off my discernment and the voice of God in my life. One day during my marriage, after that six-month period of silence, the Lord prompted me to speak up. The Holy Spirit gently ministered to me. He said, "I am losing you to that controlling and manipulative behavior coming from your husband; you are submitting to the wrong behavior. I never told you to submit to the gender of a mortal man; I told you to submit to my love. If that man is not reflecting the characteristics of My love, you are not obligated to subject yourself to abusive behavior. You are doing so as an irrelevant sacrifice for My name's sake." The Spirit of the Lord told me that His love does not look like that. He said, "Shicreta, your husband is using the credibility of the Bible to justify his controlling behavior. This is not okay. You must speak up and tell him that I said he is illegally using the Bible to justify his abusive, oppressive, and disrespectful behavior toward you as a woman." Basically, God was telling me that He had never given mortal men preeminence over women. After all, if God had given preeminence to men, He would not bother to rebuke them for bad behavior. They would have a pass regardless of what they did. However, when God spoke to me, His words said otherwise.

Well, of course, after I heard the Lord speak to me, I did exactly what the Lord had asked. I told my husband what the Lord had spoken to me. I let him know that he was illegally using the Bible to cover his bad behavior. When I told him what the Lord had said, he had no idea what to say; he just stood there, but he never completely stopped mistreating me. He just slowed down to regroup his devious ways. His behavior toward me was still atrocious; he just tried to hide his true colors by finding a more cunning way to control and abuse me. It's true that not every part of my relationship with my ex-husband was horrible. His strong work ethic, organizational skills, and craftsmanship were greatly appreciated, as were many other things he did well. Although he would apologize throughout the marriage, he never really showed any signs that he was willing to do whatever it took to change and work on our relationship. Truthfully, I know my ex did not wake up one day and set out to destroy the life of another human being. I feel as though in his life he experienced negativity that he allowed to trap his soul under the curse of Eve. I believe that he tried to love me using the only form of misguided love he knew about and was conscious of. I know I'm not perfect and that I did not do everything right in my marriage. However, one thing I can honestly say, regardless of how my husband treated me, is that I chose to love and respect him no matter what—which, toward the end, even he acknowledged. Throughout my situation, I sought counsel, prayed earnestly, and made every effort to communicate, all while trying to save an abusive marriage and feeling like a lone warrior at the expense of my own wounded soul. However, in spite of all the emotional wounds he inflicted, I chose to look at him through the eyes of mercy. I realized that I could not expect him to give me love when it was evident that he did not have any for himself. How could he give me something he did not have? As I learn more about the effects of the curse, this knowledge has made it much easier for me to forgive my ex-husband for hurting me, stoning me, and emotionally discarding me like I was a disposable item.

Torn Perception

Well, after hearing the words that the Lord had spoken to me, I saw and heard the heart of God in a way that I had never seen or heard it before. What I heard went against all that I had been taught within the Christian church. Based on what I heard the Lord speak to me, what I read in the Bible, and what I had been taught within the Christian church, I began to test the spirit and source behind the voice. For a while, I was a bit confused. During that time, I started to question everything I believed about God and His true order for males and females within marriage. Once I transitioned out of that relationship and pressed through the heartbreak and pain that came with the abuse and divorce, as I looked back over my relationship, I was able to clearly see that my ex- husband's disrespectful attitude and abusive behavior had been based solely on the overall belief and interpretation of the teachings within the Christian church that clearly elude to the fact that God created and established men to rule over women. These writings clearly portray the woman as being subjugated by the husband; then they place the husband on the same level as a god over the woman. In essence, according to this model, God forces the woman to give a mortal man her portion of the dominion that God has given to her. So, what God has given to the woman is now silenced, disregarded, disrespected, and ruled over by a mortal man as her superior.

Reflection of Beliefs

As I explained in the first chapter, a person's perception is birthed from the roots of what one believes. Within the Christian church, or any other religion, a person acquires what they believe from repetitive teachings on the same subject. Overall, regardless of what one believes is positive or negative, whatever a person believes is what that person will perceive and live out. For example, whether or not a person agrees with the transgender lifestyle, that person cannot change the fact that God created humanity with a free will that God or the devil cannot control. A person is either going to choose to believe in Christ and change, or confess to know Christ in error and remain the same. For instance, if a man sets his mind to believe that he is a woman, he will do everything in his power to reflect that which he believes and make it a part of his life. Regardless of the fact that God did not create him to be a woman, that man's goal is to birth what he believes, making his perception of himself a visible part of his life. Whether a person agrees or disagrees with the actions of a transgender person, that person was created to make a choice. Adam and Eve were given the same choice. What one does with the choice one is given is up to that person, but in the end, God will either approve or disapprove of one's heart motives and actions. The essence of every person is reflected in what they believe. Based on what I have experienced and been taught within the Christian church, I find it unsurprising that I allowed myself to be abused in the name of God, to assume that I was honoring Him by staying and praying my way through. So, although the Christian church claims that these verses describe the "role" of a male and not the "sex" of a male, my question is: Why do many commentaries, Bible teachings, and counseling sessions point to and encourage the woman to submit to her husband as the essence of the male sex being superior to the woman? To me, the role of a man can be suspended or removed, but the essence of the male gender is grafted into the man; it reflects what a man believes and perceives himself to be. When a man is born, one specific part of his body determines his sex. It can be altered and he may try to change it, but the essence of the male gender and personality that God created will always remain. So, if the interpretation of Ephesians is all that men and women within the Christian church are raised to believe, that interpretation is all they will ever know and, therefore, all that they will ever live out. A large majority of leaders, both male and female, within the Christian church encourage these beliefs regardless of the man's behavior. Due to this reality, there have been innumerable married Christian women who, in an effort to save their marriages, have sought Christian counsel. Unfortunately, the true beliefs engraved into the heart of the majority of the Christian church tell these women to simply submit to and pray for their husbands no matter what and to continue doing whatever their husbands say because that is God's order. As a woman, I had been trained to believe these passages were to be followed as superior to God's original order. This is the main reason why I remained quiet and allowed my husband to abuse and disrespect me for as long as I did. Sadly, many Christian women stay much longer than I did, thinking that they, too, are doing God a service.

Role vs. Gender

As I said in a previous chapter, although there are more women leaders within the Christian church today than there were 100 or even 50 years ago, for centuries the majority of the leaders within the Christian church were male. Because men within the Christian church have been the predominant leaders, they have been the ones to teach these passages from Ephesians as if the words were merely reflective of the male as being one whom God commissioned to uphold the "role" of superior leadership over women. They teach all the Bible passages I mentioned as if God "created" the man to rule over the woman and as if God commanded the woman to submit and respect the role of leadership that God "created" for the man. They teach these passages as if what the writer said was the foundation and primary order that God originally established for all marital relationships. The message that the verses in Ephesians spell out is evident, the overall position of the man in the marriage relationship is perceived through a mindset that comes only from the curse of Eve. In essence, this places man in a superior position to that of a woman, just as Christ is superior to His church. The message they "say" is being relayed is innocent and reflective of God's order. However, in reality, based on what is taught through the perception of the curse of Eve, once a woman marries her husband, he essentially becomes her ruler. Whatever ability the woman had to listen to God is dismissed; now she is to look to her husband for all knowledge, wisdom, protection, and guidance. According to these verses in Ephesians, the woman submits everything to the man, but God never commands the man to submit to or even respect the woman. For many women, no matter what the Christian church "says" about the innocent role of the man in a marriage, based on the extremely high number of female victims of domestic abuse and the countless women who have lost their lives while trying to follow these teachings within the Christian church, I would say that the actual message that is believed and being conveyed is much different from simply respecting and honoring the "role" of the man. Most women who genuinely love God aim to obey His word. In doing so, many women do as I once did. We end up allowing our husbands to dictate and control our relationships with God, as well as what we can and cannot do. Most women (myself included) allow and put up with abusive behaviors from men. Sadly, many women (myself included) think that they are obeying God by letting the man lead them, even if it is to the woman's detriment. No matter what the Christian church "says" they believe, the evidence of what they believe is being lived out through the extremely high number of female victims of domestic abuse all over the world. Because these writings are the most popular Biblical passages used to establish the standings for both Christian and non-Christian male and female relationships, I would say that regardless of what many within the Christian church "say" they believe about the "role" of a man, it is evident that they believe that the "gender" of a man is superior to that of a woman, as this model is reflective only of the curse of Eve and not at all reflective of God's original order, which He sent through Jesus Christ. If what I am saying does not reflect reality, why does most Bible reference material indicate that the male is superior to the female and command the female to be the only one in the relationship to submit and respect the husband? Before my abusive marriage, I thought that God really did place the male gender over me. However, then I realized that this did not add up to what God had established as His original order before the fall.

General Request

What I find interesting is that, to the majority of the Christian church, the slanted message in Ephesians 5:22-25, 33 seems to outweigh the very clear message of mutual love and respect written in Ephesians 5:1-2 and 19-21. However, one thing I notice is that when it comes to any verse being shared in reference to marriage, mutual respect, love, and submission, those verses are always dismissed and shut down with arguments that say those verses don't apply to marriage. Ephesians 5:1-2, says, *"Therefore be imitators of God as dear children. And walk in love, as Christ also has loved us and given Himself for us, an offering and a sacrifice to God for a sweet-smelling aroma."* Then, in chapter 5:19-21, *"...speaking to one another in psalms and hymns and spiritual songs, singing and making melody in your heart to the Lord, giving thanks always for all things to God the Father in the name of our Lord Jesus Christ, submitting to one another in the fear of God."*

Now, these verses encourage mutual respect and love among all Christians, including all general male and female relationships. However, somehow, whoever wrote Ephesians 5:22-25, 33 completely disregarded the equality that requires the male and female to love, respect, and submit to one another. What I find interesting is that the word "submit" in verses 21-22 is derived from the Greek word "Hupotasso," which means *to arrange under, to subordinate, to subject, put in subjection, to subject one's self, obey, to submit to one's control, to yield to one's admonition, or advice, to obey, be subject.* The word itself means the same in both forms of use. Yet somehow, based on today's perception of these verses, the marriage model reflects what is actually a one-sided relationship that literally strips the woman of the essence of the liberated rights that Christ shed His blood to restore to her. The model taught and believed by many within the Christian Church today places the woman back under the curse of Eve as being inferior to the superior position of the man.

The Essence of Submission

Because I have been liberated to see the love of God through Christ perception, I realize that submission in itself is not evil; it is actually a trait found in the Trinity. Considering that both males and females were created in God's image, it is a trait that is naturally found in both men and women who have been reconciled back to God through Jesus Christ. Jesus Himself was submissive to God His Father until His death. John 5:19 says, *"Then Jesus answered and said to them, 'Most assuredly, I say to you, the Son can do nothing of Himself, but what He sees the Father do; for whatever He does, the Son also does in like manner.'"* This verse is a great example of how Jesus showed Himself as being submissive, as doing and saying what God asked Him to do and say. Now, here it is: Jesus is a man and He showed Himself to be submissive, but yet, the majority of the Christian Church omits Jesus and sets the male sex on the same level as Jesus. Then, in turn, they demand that the woman submit to the man with no reciprocation. Truth be told, submission is all about attitude. My definition of submission is to show oneself as considerate, respectful, and not so strong-willed as to always do what one wants but instead to sometimes be open to doing what someone else desires. In a relationship, unless one is literally "God," submission goes both ways, not just one way. God is the only one who requires full submission from those who follow Him through Christ; no human being, male or female, has been given that right by God, and no human being will ever be given that right. Technically, the only other person who will demand a form of one-sided submission is the anti- Christ being possessed by Satan. In the area of general submission, whoever wrote these passages was on point;

that perception should have been carried into the marriage as God Himself originally established it. The same passage of scripture, Ephesians 5:31, shows the correct perception that God originally authorized in Genesis 2:23-24 for the marriage relationship. Ephesians 5:31 says, *"For this reason a man shall leave his father and mother and be joined to his wife, and the two shall become one flesh."* This verse reflects the proper order of relationships by repeating what God said in the beginning, in Genesis 2:23-24 before the fall. Jesus also made that statement in Mark 10:7-8. However, the majority of the Christian church seems to operate so much under the curse of Eve that it cannot see anything more than the fallen superior image of man ruling over the public forum of the Christian church and serving as the model for their relationships. The reality is, God has and will always be about mutual submission, love, respect, and equality within a marriage and within the overall public environment of the Christian church. (We will discuss Genesis 2:23-24 in much more detail in Chapter 11.)

CHAPTER 9

HEART VS. WORD

As a child growing up, I used to think that the Bible had been dropped from heaven by God and, miraculously, found its way to the store where it was sold. However, as I mentioned in Chapter 1, that is far from the reality of how the Bible's physical contents were actually compiled. To help you understand a bit more about what may have happened with the verses I reviewed in Chapters 7 and 8, let me take a minute to explain something about the Bible. It is a proven fact that because the Bible is a translated book, certain words and passages may not fully reflect what was intended. For example, "church" was not originally a word used in the Bible. Years ago, when the Bible went through another translation process, the word "church" was used to replace the original translated word "congregation." The word "congregation" was originally used in William Tyndale's version of the Bible, which was created before the popular King James Version. As a matter of fact, a large majority of William Tyndale's version was used during that process. "Congregation" was originally used to reflect the original Greek word Ekklesia (which means "the called out ones"). Interestingly, the words "church" and "congregation" have completely different meanings in terms of what they represent, but I will address that in much greater detail in another book. We can also see the added English words *thee, thou, shalt, sayest, yea*, etc. as showing that the King James Version of the Bible was translated by English bishops and scholars of the Protestant and Catholic Churches in England way back in the 16th century. Plus, when it comes to the writers of the Bible, we must understand that almost every situation that the Apostles addressed in the New Testament was based on instructions provided for specific situations at that time in history. To really understand the Bible, one must study and learn Bible history. One must learn what was going on at the time when a specific passage was written, which parts of what was written truly reflect God's heart for His people today, how the content restores a vision of God's original plan from the beginning before the fall, and the specific instructions given for that time that we can carry into today. For example, we know that 1 Corinthians 6:9-10, 1 Timothy 9-10, Romans 1:18-32, etc., are all verses that describe the sins (behaviors) that God's heart and character reject. Therefore, because the nature and heart of God is righteous and His character cannot accept sinful behaviors, we know that those verses truly reflect God's original order as seen through Christ perception. Each recorded sin breaks and destroys God's original order for our relationship with Him and our relationships with one another.

Here is another example. Many Christians tend to embrace everything written in the Old Testament. However, not every commandment in the Old Testament is intended to be followed today. For example, the fact that God commanded the Jews to sacrifice animals and to give agricultural tithes and offerings to the Jewish priest in a temple does not require today's gentile (non-Jewish) Christians to follow those same instructions. It would be totally weird if Christians started bringing animals, grain, or monetary tithes and offerings into a modern-day Christian church as if it were a Jewish temple where Christian leaders have somehow been miraculously reincarnated into Jewish priests. I mean, seriously, how funny would it be if you arrived at a Sunday morning service in America and you saw a line of people with lambs on leashes and birds in cages or with fistfuls of money in the palms of their hands, all waiting on their chance to receive a blessing that Christ already gave. Now, don't get me wrong; if a person gives monetary gifts to a Christian church, that's fine, but to follow the commandments of God's former instructions as if God still commanded the public system of the church to receive a specific amount of money as a mandatory requirement is, well, not truly relevant to the reason why Christ came. (I will discuss the liberation of Jesus Christ in further detail in Chapter 12.)

Although the Mosaic laws command that a person should be stoned for breaking specific sins, Christians today should not follow those laws and physically stone people. Basically, when Jesus went against the written word by not stoning the woman caught in adultery, He was taking a stance for the heart of God that was superior to God's previous words. In the case of the verses we read in Chapters 7 and 8 (1 Timothy, 1 Corinthians, and Ephesians), we can see that based on perception and maybe even information that could have been lost in translation, these verses clearly do not reflect God's original order of unity that He created males and females to walk in. So, simply by pointing out these evident facts, we should see how important it is for people to learn God's heart and His character, and not just follow a word that has God's name on it without knowing His heart, without understanding God's original intentions for humanity. Today, with so many different translations of the Bible being written and so many verses of the Bible being changed or even removed, it seems to be getting more difficult for people to see the character of God and His heart that He sent through Jesus Christ. When a person follows the words of God without connecting to the heart of God, his or her mind will remain imprisoned by the curses of Adam and Eve. The person will hope that his or her deeds are good enough to be accepted by God. I like what Paul said in 2 Corinthians 3:6: *"Who also made us sufficient as ministers of the new covenant, not of the letter but of the Spirit; for the letter kills, but the Spirit gives life."* It is sad to see so many within the Christian church valiantly defend a written word while treating people— especially women—so heartlessly. I can go on and on with examples, but ultimately this is why the Bible says, in 2 Timothy 2:15, *"Be diligent to present yourself approved to God, a worker who does not need to be ashamed, rightly dividing the word of truth."* Simply by understanding those facts, we can see that the intended essence can be mistakenly lost, either innocently (through the addition of useless words in translation), due to mistranslation, or because the person who is reading the text is misperceiving what is being said. Also, the presentation of the text can be affected by what was happening at the time when the passages were written. These are all factors to keep in mind when reading the Bible.

Holy Confusion

I have noticed that two verses in the Bible are greatly misunderstood and tend to cause a lot of confusion among many Christians. Those verses are 2 Timothy 3:16-17, which says, *"All Scripture is given by inspiration of God, and is profitable for doctrine, for reproof, for correction, for instruction in righteousness, that the man of God may be complete, thoroughly equipped for every good work."* Now, based on these verses, it appears that every word in the Bible is considered to be holy to God and that all the words in the Bible are to be followed by those who follow God. However, while the words in the Old and New Covenants were inspired by God, when Jesus came, a whole new perception of God was established. Yes, God spoke to Moses and commanded Him to write the Old Covenant laws. Yes, it is also true that God sent His Son to the earth as a living embodiment of His words in human form to connect and restore humanity back to its rightful place of Righteousness in God. And, yes, it is likewise true that the Holy Spirit communicated a lot of His words to the New Testament Apostles. However, not every word inspired by God is to be followed today because not every word in the Bible is inspired by the same perception of God. This is a truth that Jesus reflected in His life. We saw this reality when Jesus encountered the woman who had been caught in adultery. We also saw this renewed perception when Jesus allowed His disciples to defy Jewish customs by eating with unwashed hands (Matthew 15:1-11). What we must understand is that some words in the Bible are inspired by God's former Old Covenant order, which was written under the curses of Adam and Eve. Meanwhile, other words in the Bible were truly inspired by God's New Order, which was sent through Jesus Christ. So, in essence, some of the words are veiled through the curses of Adam and Eve and some of the words are active and alive in Christ. As I said at the beginning of this book, the Bible was written using two very different perceptions. Truthfully, the perception of the person who is reading it as well as the perception of God from the writer will determine on which side of inspiration the passage falls—the same inspiration, but two different perceptions and sets of instructions. The main thing that matters when reading the Bible is truly aiming our hearts to learn the nature, heart, and character of God sent through Christ perception. Sadly, if we aim to follow everything in the Bible, we end up terribly confused and still mentally veiled by the curses of Adam and Eve, all while holding a Bible in our hands. Consequently, we weigh ourselves down so much that we fall prey to religion, and the joy of our salvation no longer exists.

The Words of Christ Equal Life

As I have previously stated, the Bible is often misperceived and misunderstood. When Jesus caught the woman in adultery, He did not embarrass or demean her. He protected her from physical condemnation and separated her from her sin. He did not exploit her or aim to punish her for the sin that she had committed. Instead, He released her from her sin. Just a side note: Most of the consequences that a person suffers as a result of sin are usually consequences that the person brings on themselves due to their own actions. Jesus spoke the same life-giving words to the Samaritan woman he met by the well. That woman had five husbands and yet Jesus did not embarrass her. He encouraged her to drink from His well of life, which will never run dry (John 1:1-26). Jesus spoke to the Samaritan woman and liberated her so that she could choose to have a better life with a real love that would never again leave her thirsty for the love of a mortal man. In another story, Jesus spoke life to and liberated Mary Magdalene from demonic possession and the bondage of prostitution (Luke 8:2).

The reality is, Jesus did not oppress women or set out to punish women because Eve ate of the fruit. Yet according to a large majority of the Christian church, and even according to those who wrote the passages that I discussed in Chapters

7 and 8, that is basically what happened and what is still happening. Many doctrines established since Christ's death and resurrection are still behaving as if the fall was solely Eve's fault and, sadly, are still punishing women for what Eve chose to do. In reality, while Adam may not have taken the first bite, he still chose to eat of the same forbidden fruit from which Eve chose to eat. So, in hindsight, they are both equally responsible for what happened. God knew that and held each one equally responsible for Adam and Eve's individual actions. Somehow, the majority of the Christian church seems to be addicted to perceiving women through the eyes of punishment, all because they refuse to acknowledge that Adam was just as guilty as Eve was. Neither male nor female is perfect; rather, they are fragile human beings who equally need God's love and acceptance. This is why it is so sad to see many Christian men believe that they are somehow the only ones responsible for answering to God for their wives. God did not place a mortal man in that position. God holds both the male and the female responsible for what they do in a relationship and in their individual personal lives. The wife is just as responsible for loving and respecting her husband as the husband is for loving and respecting his wife because, in the end, God is looking at their hearts. God will be looking for the reflection of His Son's love in the hearts of both the male and the female. Contrary to popular belief in a large ma-

jority of the Christian church, a mortal man is not divine and will not receive a "pass" from God simply because he is a man. He will be held accountable for his behavior, just like the woman will be held accountable for hers. It is so sad to see many beautiful people within the Christian church remove the heart of God sent through Christ and settle under the curse of Eve, all while speaking words from the Bible that clearly do not reflect God's original order, which He sent Christ to restore. The truth is, while the heart and character of God will never change, some of the words in the Bible have been changed several times— and are still being changed. However, the changes that have been made in some versions of the Bible are small in comparison to the heart and character of God sent through Christ, which has always remained the same.

I used to follow and believe the very verses that I shared in Chapters 7 and 8. Then, one day, I saw the heart of God sent through Jesus, and He truly restored my perception of God's original order. Thankfully, I now believe in God's original order, which situates God as our only true and divine King. Now I know that God created men and women to be human beings who are joined together as one, side by side under the umbrella of God's love.

The "I Am" Preceded the Written Word

Although I know that I have made some surprising yet verifiable accusations about the Bible, I do not believe that I have discounted its relevance in any way. Long before the Bible existed, men like Noah, Abraham, Isaac, Moses, and so many others had no scriptures to which they could turn. The only reality that Moses knew about God was that He called Himself I AM; he knew nothing else. Yet, God chose each person before the Mosaic laws were ever written. Why did God choose them? Because they had faith to believe that there was only one God who represented the essence of what is Good, Holy, Righteous, Just, and True. All they had was faith in the ambiance of God's loving character, to which they responded through obedient acts of love for God and His people. The Bible is a book that is full of revelations God spoke through multiple individuals. The spoken and living (Greek word "Rhema") *words* of God were captured in writing and became the written (Greek word "Logos") *word* of God that everyone reads today. Once God's Holy Spirit brings His "Rhema" words to life in each person who sees God through Christ, He will help us see and recognize God's character sent through Jesus Christ within the words we read. In reality, the curse of Eve has two sides; however, I will wait until my next book to expose the other side. Do you think that God would want His people to be delivered only halfway by only acknowledging that Christ broke the curse of Adam, or delivered all the way by acknowledging that Christ broke the curse of Eve as well? Knowing God as the loving Father whom He is, I believe that He would want His followers to know the full truth and nothing but His spoken "Rhema" living truth.

God's Heart Will Never Change

All the new translations of the Bible are starting to differ so much that the essence of who God is and what He stands for is being lost. People have taken God's inspired word and further removed Christ perception in an effort to pass all unnatural sinful relationships that God deems unfruitful, as if God were okay with it. People really think they can change the heart of God by changing His words, but God is much more than His word. A person can change the words in the Bible, but they can never change God's heart and character. His word was in existence long before it was ever written, and the character and heart of God are what hold His words. It is crucial that we understand the foundation of God's loving heart and character in which the Bible was written. For instance, today there is a version of the Bible that calls people names like "potato head" and "stupid." However, suppose that someone who reads this version has been raised in an abusive home where they were called bad names all their life.

How is a person going to heal if they think that God is calling them names as well? We call ourselves "stupid" or "dumb" for the crazy things we do, but that doesn't mean God demeans us or calls us out of our names. The Bible will always be a book associated with God, and Satan knows that the best way to keep people in confusion is to exalt the curse of Eve, which prevents God's people from connecting to God's heart and seeing God's character sent through Jesus Christ. The followers of Christ are supposed to test every Spirit and follow only every word that proceeds out of the mouth of Christ. They are not supposed to simply take every word that comes in His name without His heart and character. At the end of the day, the one aspect of God that can never be manipulated, controlled, or changed is the relationship boundaries that reflect the character of His love, which was exemplified through His Son, Jesus Christ, and the essence of His loving nature that encompasses the totality of who He is. The true character of God will always produce fruitfulness and life-giving relationships. To know Him is to know fruitfulness. To know Him is to know liberation and life. To know God is to know His order for all humanity. To know God is to accept His Son, Jesus Christ. To know God is to know love. When one truly knows God, unity between men and women is reflected with mutual submission, love, and respect.

CHAPTER 10

CIRCUS MASTER'S

After being a part of the Christian church for so long, I have noticed that the core beliefs of most of the Christian Church are terribly off-center. We know that perception is birthed from belief. Therefore, the damage that has been done to women, the oppression to which women have been subjected, and the inexcusable abusive behavior of many men within the Christian church show that their belief is not rooted in Jesus Christ. Due to our inability to see Christ, our teachings and doctrines are cold and oppressive toward women. This is also why the male sex is over-exalted above where God created him to be. Sadly, during many Sunday morning services, I seldom hear teachings about God through Christ perception.

It seems as though, during Sunday morning service, while I hear the name of Jesus a lot, I rarely see the loving and respectful character and nature of God that Jesus represented. When people do not see God through the eyes of what Jesus did, many of the leaders within the Christian church convey messages filled with misrepresentations and half-truths about what God expects from men and women. Most of the misperceptions I have heard within the Christian church damage the relationships between God and humanity and men and women rather than help humanity unite with God and help the sexes unite with one another. These misrepresentations sometimes feel as though they are pumped into my veins like a drug, on a continual basis with no end.

Groomed for Destruction

When I was growing up, my parents watched a famous Christian TV network. On that network, many different ministers preached what was supposed to be the doctrine of Christ. However, not every doctrine taught on that network or during Sunday morning services truly reflected God's heart and character sent through Jesus Christ. Instead, many of those teachings that I heard growing up were poisonous to my overall growth in Christ. Instead of representing God according to the essence of His character, they seemed to exalt all the differences between the genders. They also used science to validate their misrepresentations and prove that God created men and women to be broken. One major misrepresentation of God that affects the overall growth of men, as taught within the Christian Church, is the lie that alludes to a false reality that God "created" men to be "prideful" and to have a "superior ego" equal to God, and that God "created" women to praise and stroke men's egos. These doctrines were taught as if they were God's order and as if He expected and approved of the superior and prideful status of man. In reality, God rebukes pride and a superior attitude and demands humility from all His followers—male and female. James 4:5-8 says:

> "Or do you think that the Scripture says in vain, 'The Spirit who dwells in us yearns jealously'? But He gives more grace. Therefore, He says: 'God resists the proud, but gives grace to the humble.' Therefore, submit to God. Resist the devil and he will flee from you. Draw near to God and He will draw near to you. Cleanse your hands, you sinners; and purify your hearts, you double-minded.

Also, Psalms 16:18-19 says:

"Pride goes before destruction, and a haughty spirit before a fall. It is better to be of a lowly spirit with the poor than to divide the spoil with the proud."

To God, pride is pride. He will never excuse a prideful look and superior attitude among men or women. Jesus does not wink at the superior attitude that many men within the Christian church are trained to maintain. Yet, to a large majority of Christians, as long as the man is going to church and confessing to know God, his prideful and superior attitude is excused. If the man is a leader within an organization, his prideful behavior is celebrated, and he is looked up to as if he were a god. Truthfully, when it comes to who is praised in a relationship, both men and women should show their praise, appreciation, and gratitude toward one another equally.

Another misrepresentation of God that is taught within the Christian church and that has caused so much disrespect for women, as well as left many men in a very weak and troubled state, is a Christian teaching that says God "created" men to be visual creatures—visually stimulated only by what their natural eyes see as they gaze upon a woman's body. The key word in each of these teachings is "created." These teachings indicate that God purposed men to be that way. They say that God is okay with it. In essence, these teachings excuse men's disrespect and lustful eyes directed toward a woman's body, indicating that they are the norm. However, when Jesus came, He said something totally different from what the majority of Chris-tian doctrines teach. In Matthew 5:28, Jesus said, *"But I say to you that whoever looks at a woman to lust for her has already committed adultery with her in his heart."* In this verse, Jesus is rebuking the men for having lustful eyes to-ward women. He rebuked men because, historically, through-out the Old Testament, men had the upper hand and were the ones who received the right to pick and choose women using the instructions that God gave. History shows that men rarely followed the monogamous guidelines that God origi-nally established in the beginning before the fall. The reality is, if God actually "created" men to be visually stimulated, driven solely by their sight or their imagination about a wom-an's body, why would Jesus go against His Father's created order and rebuke the lust of a man's eye? Furthermore, why does 2 Corinthians 10:5 encourage us to, *"Cast down imag-inations, and every high thing that exalteth itself against the knowledge of God, and bringing into captivity every thought to the obedience of Christ;"*

Another point I want to make is that if God created men to habitually lust after women with unsatisfied, wandering eyes, what is the excuse for gay men? Did God make them that way, too? Did God create some men to lust after women and some men to lust after men? Or could it be that the curses of Adam and Eve have made us all sick, creating lustful, unchaste men, some who lust after women and some who lust after men? The reality is that lust is lust, no matter who is lusting. Unrestrained burning sexual desires are the same for both men and women. Once we understand that Jesus came to reestablish His Father's original order, which was given before the fall, we also understand that God did not "create" men to be driven by visual stimulation and to be overly infatuated with the female body to the point that they habitually disrespect another human being. However, this is what many men within the Christian church are raised to believe about themselves. Sadly, those beliefs destroy the bonds of trust between women and men and cause many women to have continual trust issues with men.

Although it is true that lust is a weakness of the flesh for both men and women, in the beginning, God did not handcraft that weakness into Adam or Eve. Men were not created to be lustful. The picture I get of Adam in the glimpse that I see from the beginning is nothing like what many Christian doctrines portray. Adam was a man of purpose focused on walking in the dominion that God had given him. He was neither running around like an uncontrollable dog in heat nor obsessed with being horny, begging God to put someone there to satisfy his sexual urges and desires. Nope, not at all. Adam was way too busy loving and obeying God.

God saw that Adam was alone and He wanted to bless him with a mate comparable to him—someone comparable to his chasteness, self-discipline, perception, vision, goals, etc. God did not want to see Adam alone. Yet, sadly, under many of today's doctrines, men are literally preached into defeat. Many men within the Christian church are forced into mental prisons, banished from the full perception of the new identity of their relationship with God sent through Jesus Christ. Based on the overall lust and disrespect that women face within the Christian church every day, I would say: How can a man teach another man his identity in Christ if many male leaders within the Christian church don't know their original identity? I guess this is where Jesus would say that the blind lead the blind right into a ditch (Matthew 15:14). So, if one does not know his original identity, how can he teach someone else theirs? The truth is, all men and women have eyes; we all can recognize when a person looks good. When looking for a mate respectfully, one looks for someone to whom they are attracted. However, it is unacceptable to excuse the behavior of a man who habitually disrespects women with his eyes to the point that he is unfaithful to the one he is with. When a man seeks a woman for nothing more than a one-time sexual experience, that is not okay; God will never be fine with that behavior. Women are human beings; we are more than a notch on some Christian or non-Christian guy's wall. Both inside and outside the Christian church, as women, we are used, abused, and disrespected. We are objects who have been taught that God basically created us to be bought, sold, ruled over, and conquered. The only difference with men outside the Christian church is that the men within the Christian church, especially many of the leaders, use the Bible to hide behind and justify their behavior as if God were okay with it.

The other misrepresentation I have noticed is that women are taught that God created them to be emotional. This excuses a woman's over-emotionalism. It tells her that God created males to rule over her because her unstable emotions cause her to make poor decisions. This is not a Christ-centered teaching. The Bible tells both women and men to submit their emotions to God's Holy Spirit, which lives within us. We are not supposed to habitually allow our unresolved emotions to dominate our lives and affect our life choices on any level (Colossians 3:14-15; Galatians 5:16-18). However, knowing this truth does not dismiss the human moments that we all have. During those times, we must show compassion for ourselves, just like we do for everyone else.

Holy Narcissists

Sadly, I have heard more than one story from women who have had bad experiences with male leaders within the Christian church. On a typical Sunday morning, the women would enter the service, dressed in flattering yet modest clothing. Some women would wear sleeveless blouses and maybe skirts that hit a little above the knees, while others would wear form-fitting yet flattering clothes. Some women would wear sexy, revealing clothes. In each case, the male leaders would notice the ladies' clothing from the pulpit, then get beside themselves and become distracted. After service, the men would go to the women and literally chastise them for wearing clothes that the men deemed to be seductive. In some cases, the men would misuse their authority and sexually assault or even rape the women. In each case, the leaders claimed that the women's choice of dress caused them to lust. The leaders would literally treat the women as if they were lepers who had sinned against God by causing the men to stumble into sin. Those leaders were basically blaming the women for their problem with lust. Sadly, those lust-obsessed leaders told the women that they had a spirit of seduction, and that their clothes were causing them to sin and lust.

Unfortunately, the women who shared their stories with me were hurt and discouraged. They felt dirty and thought they had done something really bad to sin against God. A few of the women became so broken about the lustful behavior on the part of male leaders that they started wearing baggy clothes, long dresses, and long-sleeved shirts simply to avoid attention from men. Some never wanted to step foot in any organized institution within the Christian church again.

Recently, while I was watching Aretha Franklin's funeral, Ariana Grande performed "Natural Woman." After her performance, the bishop presiding over the funeral held Ariana's body very close while telling her an innocent joke about her name. Although the joke was actually funny and even Ariana laughed, something was happening with the bishop's hand. To my surprise, his hand was literally pressed against the side of her breast. It looked as if his fingers were going in for a mammogram. It was a bit uncomfortable to watch, and judging by the look on Ariana's face, I don't think she knew what to do. Whether intentional or not, the bishop's hand held ground. It wasn't spiritual ground, and he wasn't holding up his hand to pray. Thankfully, he showed character by making a public apology in a very sincere and kind way; to me, it seemed very authentic. His attitude about the situation showed me that some male leaders within the Christian church can actually take responsibility for their bad behavior and not blame Satan or the woman for their mistakes.

Yet the majority of the Christian church blamed Ariana's attire. They accused her, as if her dress had tempted the bishop to touch her inappropriately. The day after the funeral, so many people on social media, mostly Christians, were condemning Ariana for attending a church service wearing such a short skirt. I felt so bad for Ariana because she had attended the funeral simply to show respect to the Queen of Soul and perform Aretha's song, not to join that organization or join the choir in heaven. As a woman, I understand the situation. Men have held me in the same way, either intentionally or unintentionally, and I am sure many women have been through the same type of situation. Yes, it was very uncomfortable, but I got through it with an awkward look on my face—the same one Ariana had on hers. Technically, for a believer in Christ, when it comes to how a person lives or dresses, it is all based on the conviction of the Holy Spirit, not on the misaligned judgments of so many dysfunctional people within the Christian church—people who seem to spend more time concerned about how a person dresses than about the condition of that person's heart and soul. What kind of image is that for Ariana and her 20-something generation? Sadly, now she probably sees the church environment as judgmental, and she may see God as one who condones judgmental and lustful behaviors.

What's interesting is that, in the same Bible that Christians read out of, James 1:14 says: *"But each one is tempted when he is drawn away by his own desires and enticed."* According to this verse alone (not to mention all the other verses in the Bible), each person is responsible for their own behavior. However, within a large majority of the Christian church, especially among many male church leaders, all bad behavior stems from Satan and the woman. When it comes to many male leaders, sexual trouble is caused mostly by evil "Jezebel" women whom Satan uses to seduce, tempt, and lure men. In fact, this foolishness is caused by men who have problems with lust and who misuse their positions. Unfortunately, just like Adam blamed Eve and Eve blamed the devil, most Christian men who are blinded by the curse of Eve blame the devil and women for their own unchaste behavior. The sad thing is many women within the Christian church are trained to blame themselves or other women. They change everything about themselves to correct what they do and how they dress, yet they never address the outright, atrocious, and lustful behavior of many Christian men.

God created a woman's body with curves. No matter how long a dress is, a woman's breast, backside, and hips will shine through. Some women try to hide their figures by wearing clothes that are two or three sizes too big. However, wearing bigger clothes to hide the natural shape of a woman's

141

body is not really a solution. Some women have naturally large breasts that turn a crew-neck shirt into a V-neck. Some women are blessed with large backsides, and no matter how baggy their clothes are, every pair of pants these women wear is held up on its own. Many women seem to find it safer to hide behind baggy clothes. They do this in the hopes of dropping off the radar of a lustful man's eyes. However, a change of wardrobe does not fix the problem that is rooted in the hearts and beliefs of lustful men.

Holy Clothes

There are actually entire denominations that encourage women to wear only long, baggy dresses and no make-up so that they can hide from the advances of lustful men. Years ago, I was at a book signing and promotional show for my first book when a lady approached my table. She was wearing a very nice white robe. This woman literally told me that I was going to Hell because I was wearing pants. She actually told me that if I really had the Holy Spirit, I would not be wearing pants. She indicated that I would be considered more holy to God and would not attract unrighteous attention from men. I asked the lady, "Do you really think God is more concerned with my dress than He is with the status of my heart and soul?"

I was like, *If this is her god, I don't think I want this god or her denomination to be a part of my life. If this is her god, I think the image of that god is controlling and very shallow.* To me, her god was the image of sexism. The God whom I see through the eyes and mind of Jesus Christ is not that shallow. In my opinion, many Christian denominations paint a picture of God that indicates He is concerned primarily with covering a woman's body and correcting a woman's wardrobe to protect the frail, weak, unchaste eyes of lustful men. This perception is insulting to the very nature and character of God. God is a Just God; He will unveil the curse of Eve that causes the superior mindset in men, and He will expose the issues found within their lustful hearts. Before He rebukes a woman for the way she dresses, He will rebuke the lustful eyes of men. He will then confront the inferior mindset and the roots in our hearts that cause us as women to desire a man's attention so much that we disregard our self-respect by disrobing so easily. Truthfully, if a man is chaste and has self-control, he will not be fazed by a woman wearing a shorter skirt. This is why the primary issue that is never addressed within the Christian church is the narcissistic behavior shown at the highest levels by some male leadership and many men in general within the Christian church. Yet, because the truth of God's heart is seldom taught or seen through the eyes of Christ perception, both men and women are taught to perceive God through the fallen nature of Eve. In reality, is it true that some choices of dress can be more seductive and draw the attention of a lustful man much more quickly? Absolutely. Recently, I heard an interview with a popular music artist, she was asked what advice would she give to younger artist coming up in the music industry. The artist suggested that young performers should not reveal so much and instead should leave something to the mystery of a man's mind. I would say: Leave something that will require him to make a lifetime commitment so that he has enough time to peel off every layer.

Now, in regard to myself, I don't try to hide my body from men by wearing long, baggy clothing, nor do I dress with the illusion of being "holy." I dress based on my convictions. My dress may not be acceptable to some people because it is not what they perceive as "holy." The real question is: Who gets to paint the picture of what holy attire looks like and who really knows? The Bible simply mentions modest clothing; it does not provide any more details than that. What is modest to one may be too revealing to another. At the end of the day, I believe that the Holy Spirit—not the double standards of people—is the one who convicts and brings forth change. If women enter services half-dressed, until those women are convicted by the Holy Spirit and learn a different form of fashion, the fellas are just going to have to focus on removing the lustful log in their own eyes instead of trying to remove the speck that they perceive is in the women's wardrobe. With all this said, I do believe that, as we grow as mature women of God, we should make choices that do not set out to purposely cause our brothers to stumble. Regardless, when and if the brother stumbles it is his choice to do so.

Over the years, I have observed the same inexcusable lustful behaviors from men both inside and outside the Christian Church. The only difference between the lustful behaviors of a Christian in comparison with a Non-Christian man is who each one blames for their behavior. For example, recently, a well-known secular artist came forward and made an honest confession about his unfaithfulness to his famous wife. He got counsel and sought help to discover why he chose to cheat. The guy was very honest and transparent; he even gave a public interview about it. During his interview, I did not hear him blame the "Jezebel" woman or the devil one time. However, within a large majority of the Christian Church, the story is completely different. Either the woman or the devil is the one blamed for the man's lustful behavior. What's sad is that several years ago, a pastor physically abused his wife outside a hotel in Atlanta. The abuse was so serious, the news covered the story. After everything was exposed, guess what the pastor said? He literally blamed Satan for everything. I have found that many men within the Christian

church have been raised to live contrary to how God originally created them to walk: in liberty, chastity, self-control, self-
love, self-respect, and purpose. God did not create men to be
selfish, untrustworthy, abusive, unfaithful perverts, but to be
creative and trusted leaders, warriors, fathers, and husbands.
Yet many of today's doctrines within the Christian church
seem to excuse and cover the lustful behavior of men, all in
the name of God. Sadly, because the Christian Church teaches doctrines that cover and make excuses for foolish behavior, many men remain blinded by lust while doing good deeds
and even holding positions within the public forum of the
Christian church. What a man covers and excuses, he can
never change. Unfortunately, many Christian men have been
raised to maintain the illusion of a godlike sense of themselves. That fallen perception removes the relevance of pure
human respect for women. Most Christian churches teach
dehumanizing doctrines that seem to brand men and women
as victims of God's "created" nature, which we know, after
taking a closer look at the Bible is not true at all.

The Great Masquerade

I grew up in the midst of the full gospel Charismatic Christian
church, doing everything I was taught. As I previously mentioned, at the age of 13 and again in my 30s, I was sexually
violated by a man who had helped raise me. He also held a

Bible in his hand. Even Oprah Winfrey suffered sexual abuse at the hands of male family members affiliated with a denomination within the Christian church. It seems as though the Bible is a famous book for evil-hearted men to hide behind. We can also look at Catholic priests and see how so many male leaders have molested so many boys, then turned around and kept it quiet, trying to hide their actions with no apologies and fewer legal convictions. All this abuse has taken place while these men teach from the Bible. They misuse the credibility of the Bible in a sinister attempt to take advantage of innocent people.

Recently, I heard about teenage girls being raped by their Christian Baptist youth pastors. I have also heard about several Christian pastors from various denominations in other countries who misused their position and employed the Bible to excuse their diabolical behavior. One Brazilian pastor told women that his semen was holy and blessed, and he encouraged them to drink it. A Kenyan pastor requested that women show up to service with no undergarments on. Another pastor, from a country in Africa, told single women to line up on the beach so that he could kiss their bare butts and thereby bless them to attract marriage. I could go on and on with very sad stories about how women and even small children were literally rolled over sexually, all in the name of God. The reality is God has absolutely nothing to do with any of this behavior. He did not create men to behave in a manner that is so nasty and cold-hearted. Yet, this is the current image of male behavior that often goes excused as simply being a part of Satan's plan to defame men within the Christian church. In fact, that is not true at all. Satan can only influence a person; he cannot "make" anyone do anything. Everything in life is a choice. God gave both males and females the ability to make choices. This behavior is nothing more than grown men who have lost souls, contaminated beliefs, and impure hearts. Men who behave this way have been raised to perceive themselves as being on the same level as God. They have been raised to rule over women, to take what they want from women when they want it. Unfortunately, because their gender is exalted as superior to that of women, many men are simply fulfilling what they have been inadvertently taught to believe within the Christian church. Sadly, the infestation of heartless behavior by men blinded by the curse of Eve has been regarded as the norm by the Christian church and has polluted anyone who has ever followed their teachings about relationships.

CHAPTER 11

GOD'S INTENDED PLAN

As we previously discussed, in the beginning, God had a perfect plan that He initiated long before Adam and Eve disobeyed Him and ate of the forbidden fruit. In Genesis 2:23-25, we see God's original plan:

"Then the rib which the Lord God had taken from man He made into a woman, and He brought her to the man. And Adam said: 'This is now bone of my bones, And flesh of my flesh; She shall be called Woman, Because she was taken out of Man.' Therefore, a man shall leave his father and mother and be joined to his wife, and they shall become one flesh. And they were both

naked, the man and his wife, and were not ashamed."

To me, these verses reflect the ultimate sacrifice of submission to God's plan for the family unit. It takes great submission for a man to leave the comfort of his parents' home and create a new family for himself. Technically, it takes great submission and courage for both the man and the woman to take the risk of loving and trusting one another and building a family together.

According to these verses, God never commanded the woman to be dominated by the man, and he never subjugated the man to the woman. As a matter of fact, He created man and woman to operate as "one" in the true essence of a team on the earth—walking in equal love and respect for one another. What I find interesting is that, according to God's original standards for a relationship, He established Himself as the only supreme authority to Adam and Eve. God placed both male and female under only His leadership. As I mentioned earlier, Eve never received her instructions from Adam. She received them directly from God, just like Adam did.

Was Adam created first? Absolutely. However, what does that mean for men? According to the Bible, Adam was created first, but in essence, Eve was hidden in his rib. Eve was a part of Adam long before he knew what a woman was.

I mentioned Genesis 1:26-28 in a previous chapter, but I think it is fitting to mention those verses again,

"Then God said, 'Let Us make man in Our image, according to Our likeness; let them have dominion over the fish of the sea, over the birds of the air, and over the cattle, over all the earth and over every creeping thing that creeps on the earth.' So, God created man in His own image; in the image of God He created him; male and female He created them. Then God blessed them, and God said to them, Be fruitful and multiply; fill the earth and subdue it; have dominion over the fish of the sea, over the birds of the air, and over every living thing that moves on the earth.'

As you can see in these verses, in God's original plan, He never gave Adam dominion over Eve, and He never gave Eve dominion over Adam. God also stated that Eve was made just as much in His image as Adam was.

Genesis 2:18 says, *"And the LORD God said, 'It is not good that man should be alone; I will make him a helper comparable to him.'"* Some people use this to indicate that because God made Eve from Adam, man is still intended to lead and a woman is still intended to be subjugated by man. Unfortunately, those men and women who have been raised under the curse of Eve (just as I was) would argue about this verse, tying it back to what Ephesians said. However, it still does not reflect what God originally said or did. God Himself never said that He commanded the woman to be subject to the man in any way. When it comes to the woman being comparable to Adam, it reflects oneness. What Adam did, Eve did as well, because they operated as "one." God instructed the man to leave his family, cling to his wife, and start a new family, crowning God as the only true head and leader of the family.

The Characteristics of God's Love

God is love, and those who have His heart reflect His love. The love of God carries an undeniable ambiance that encompasses His order, His boundaries, and His attributes. When a person shows habitual abusive behaviors, that person is truly blinded by the curse and can neither see God nor perceive His love. As long as an abuser can use the Bible as a means of justifying their bad behavior, they will never receive true love for themselves. Therefore, they will forever hinder and oppress those whom they declare to be weaker than they are. The characteristics of God's love appear in 1 Corinthians 13:4-7:

"Love suffers long and is kind; love does not envy; love does not parade itself, is not puffed up; does not behave rudely, does not seek its own, is not provoked, thinks no evil; does not rejoice in iniquity, but rejoices in the truth; bears all things, believes all things, hopes all things, endures all things."

When a woman or man remains in an abusive relationship, they are dismissing the order of God's love as being their standard. When an abused person blames themselves for the bad behavior of their abuser, they deny that they have been created to be loved according to God's standards of love.

Physical Traits and Attributes

Although men and women are created in the image of God, they each have their own biological and physical makeup. The biological differences between women and men are verified and proven medically. One of the differences is hormonal in nature; God created men with a large amount of testosterone, and with small amounts of progesterone and estrogen. He created women with large amounts of progesterone and estrogen, and with small amounts of testosterone. The shared traces of each other's hormones alone show that God created men and women to literally connect with one other. According to Bruce Goldman, author of the article, "Two Minds, The Cognitive Differences Between Men and Women," *"Our differences don't mean one sex or the other is better or smarter or more deserving."* The fact that there may be a small number of evident differences in the brain activity of men and women does not mean that one sex is smarter or better than the other. Women and men have different physical statures, and they have a small number of evident differences in their brain activity. The differences between men and women have been set by God as a two-piece puzzle whose pieces connect perfectly. However, when the doctrines within a large majority of the Christian Church focus so much on the differences between men and women, how can men and women grow to admire and respect each other's differences as being an addition to them both and not a subtraction? Based on how relationships are taught within the Christian Church, a woman is the only one whom "God" asks to subtract her worth and value for the worth and value of a man. Again, this does not reflect the original order of God at all.

God created men and women to resemble different attributes of Himself. In essence, the woman is an extension of the man, and the man is an extension of the woman, just like the members of Christ's body are an extension of Christ on earth. Men and women represent a unified body, not a hierarchy. Yes, it is evident that men and women have different attributes. A man seems to be more protective in nature, expressing what a woman needs, while a woman is more nurturing in nature, expressing what a man needs. Now, the fact that men and women have different attributes does not mean that a man can never be nurturing or that a woman can never be protective. For example, a single dad can have a child and tap into a woman's nurturing nature, while a single mom can have a child and tap into a man's protective nature. Neither one can fully give of the other's attributes, but they can give enough to get themselves through parenthood successfully. However, considering that God created the family unit to be united, the hole from the missing parent will, in many ways, impact the child. Until God places mentors or a spouse of the opposite sex in a person's life to fully share their attributes, that person can survive but not really thrive according to God's predestined order. We must remember that each has access to the other's attributes. After all, the attributes came from the same place—straight from God's image. Before Eve was pulled out of Adam, Adam held all attributes inside himself. In essence, so did Eve because she was hidden in Adam.

Now we know that male and female were created in God's image to live in a close relationship with God and one another. So, naturally, both males and females submit to one another under God's leadership. In reality, a married couple should discuss life choices together as a team. Imagine a basketball team with God as the coach and the husband and wife as the players. This is a proper perspective. However, a large majority of the Christian church teaches the form of a relationship as follows: God is the passive general manager, the man is the head coach whom God uses to dictate the Bible and call the shots, and the woman is the player on the team, handling all the emotional, spiritual, and physical aspects of the relationship by herself. This is usually why many women literally end up by themselves in a marriage. It is basically taught that whatever the man says is always approved by God, therefore, his words are held on the same level as God and no matter what, the woman must submit. Yet, as we know, in the beginning God neither established the man as head of the woman, nor made the woman head of the man. He created them both to walk freely in dominion on earth, joined together within the boundaries of His love.

Christ Perception for Romance

Christ's goal was not only to redeem us from sin and heal our bodies but also to restore the liberating perception of God that was present before the fall. God never intended for the model of the curse of Eve to take precedence over His original order. Truthfully, God will support only what His Son did to show unity between the genders. In reality, Jesus never left specific instructions that alluded to gender bias. This is because God never established gender bias. Because God never established it, Jesus was prevented from doing anything outside of what His Heavenly Father had ordained Him to do. Jesus submitted to the love of His Father to the end. As a matter of fact, Jesus commanded that all of His disciples were to love and respect each other equally (John 13:34). In reality, before a Christian man and woman marry, they should be disciples of Christ. Jesus said, in John 13:35: *"By this all will know that you are My disciples, if you have love for one another."* The very essence of a follower of Christ is founded on love, mutual submission, equality, and respect, as in Matthew 22:37-40. It says:

> *"Jesus said to him, 'You shall love the LORD your God with all your heart, with all your soul, and with all your mind.' This is the first and great commandment. And the second is like it: 'You shall love your neighbor as yourself.'" On these two commandments hang all the Law and the Prophets."*

Again, we see in the verses above that Jesus declared that love was the new foundation of all God's laws. The love of God sent through Christ summed up the Ten Commandments. The law of love that Jesus declared would be the only way to uphold any human relationship. If you think about it, if a person loves God, they will not create idols to replace Him. If a person loves their neighbor, that person will not steal, kill, commit adultery with, be jealous of, covet, or be envious of his or her neighbor.

Because Christ has come, God no longer regards it as acceptable to structure relationships between men and women based on His former order in the Old Testament, which is rooted in the curse of Eve. So now, any man who says that he believes in Christ and desires to have a Christ-centered healthy relationship with a woman must change his perception of women. When a man continues to perceive a woman through the eyes of the Old Order, not only is his perception rejecting Christ's standards, but he is placing his thought process about women back under the curse of Eve. When men do this, their minds and perception of God are prevented from seeing Christ and the fullness of what He has done to liberate and bring equality to both the male and female genders. For anyone who is a true believer and follower of Christ, the only foundation for relationships should be the foundation that Christ implemented to bring unity, love, and respect to both males and females.

I believe that once a man and woman see the thoughts and mind of Christ in their thought patterns, they will both have an encounter with love. The essence of the attributes that Jesus represented reflects the power of love. Once an individual man and woman learn to love themselves, they will learn to value themselves and not base their value and self-esteem on feeling superior (or not superior) to others. When it comes to roles, each should discuss their strengths and weaknesses and determine who will and will not handle the various daily duties within the relationship. For example, if a woman is not the best cook and does not enjoy preparing food, but the man loves it, he should cook their meals. A woman should never feel less than a woman simply because she is not the strongest cook. If a man is not the handiest person, but if the woman loves to work with a hammer, let her do it. The fact that a woman uses tools does not make her a man and the fact that a man does not use tools does not make him less than a man. A woman or a man should never feel less than if they are at home raising the children. This is because when a couple understands how the essence of "one" works, they are both at home and at work together. Unless the relationship is a dictatorship, a real relationship between two human beings requires two-way submission, in which each person discusses everything with their husband or wife. A relationship with secrets never reaches its full potential to go beyond surviving to thriving. In a one-sided relationship, only one person is really liberated. To build a family with two parents, each parent should be active and involved in the children's lives. The man should not be the only disciplinarian; the wife should step up to the plate as well, and vice versa. All parts of a relationship require a team effort. A true team requires at least two people, not just one person dictating to everyone else. For instance, on a basketball team, when one person makes the winning shot, the entire team wins. When one person misses the shot at the buzzer, the entire team loses. God's heart is about the unity of the family. God has never been about exalting man to a position that God never created him to have.

Love and Respect

It is sad to see the majority of the Christian church still teaching doctrines that do not line up with God's restored order, which He established through Christ. Why does it seem so hard for the majority of the Christian church to simply teach women and men to love, respect, and submit to one another? What bothers me the most, as a Christian woman, is that it seems so hard for many Christians to understand that both men and women deserve mutual submission, love, respect, and equality. Many Christians get so caught up in the writings of Christ's servants, like the Apostle Paul and all the other known and unknown writers, they completely forget about the foundational standards declared by the One whom they are supposed to serve. Sadly, if you ask some Christians, "What is God's plan for marriage?", few will tell you what Jesus did or what God ordained. However, they will tell you what Paul and all the other writers said. I think the "Paulian" church, rather than the "Christian" church, would be a more suitable name. The last I checked, to be called a Christian, one must see God's order in the beginning and follow God's character sent through Jesus Christ. I think Aretha Franklin said it best: Both men and women simply need love and R.E.S.P.E.C.T.

CHAPTER 12

REALITY OF THE FALLEN

Some women express their emotions differently from some men. The main reason I am not saying "everyone" and pointing out only "some" men and women is that I have learned that the culture of our society reflects our fallen nature, and that every man and woman is usually clumped together and generalized as being and thinking the same. Both men and women are dictated to and told whom they are and what they are supposed to be. Most of the time, in research, a minority is selected and observed. Then the majority is judged based on the results of that minority. An individual man and woman must discover their likes, dislikes, strengths, and weaknesses. However, based on a very narrow view, a man is told that he is not supposed to communicate, while the woman is told that she is the communicator. Throughout their lives, they mostly emulate what they have been taught to believe about themselves. Men don't talk because they have been told that they don't do that, while women do. For example, if a man is raised to communicate and express his emotions, and if a woman is raised not knowing how to communicate, each individual will grow up and reflect what they were taught regardless of their gender. In my opinion, the reality of our fallen nature removes individualism and creates a world of robots that all think alike. For example, as I have said, many men—both inside and outside the Christian church—behave the same way because of the curse of Eve, which confines their thought patterns to a superior state, leaving them very selfish and controlling. What they think and believe about God, themselves, and women is highly distorted. Under the curse, men gravitate toward power and control, which they require to feed their superior nature. Sadly, due to the fallen state, both men and women are easily influenced and controlled by the information that sociology and research studies provide. These studies confirm the state of the fallen nature, but they are not supposed to reflect the new nature of men and women who are being transformed by thinking according to the nature of God seen only through Christ perception.

Damsel in Distress

Women who are blinded by the curse of Eve seem to live in a constant state of needing to be rescued by a man. Due to the inferior state of the woman, she feels like she is bound to needing and constantly desiring a man. She lives her life as though she can never be complete without a man. Sadly, no matter how that man treats her, she will often remain in a broken relationship because, to her, being with a broken man is better than being alone without a man to cover and console her inferior emotions. A woman who thinks under the curse lives bound to doing anything she can to gain a man's attention. A woman will decrease the amount of her clothing, abandon her self-worth, and subject herself to doing things she is not comfortable with, just to gain a man's attention. In essence, due to the curse, a woman is bound to needing a man's approval and attention to feel satisfied with herself. Most women under the curse don't know how to love and respect themselves on their own. This is why so many men can use sex as a means of luring women. A man can make a woman "feel" love when he is getting what he wants from her. When a woman "feels" love, even if the feelings of love from that man are not real, the illusions of her emotions will cause her to give that man her everything. Sadly, many of us women who are blinded by the curse literally feel emotional connections to abusive men. Many of us struggle to break those connections. When we as women are bound by the thoughts that stem from the curse of Eve, we are literally bound to desire a man to rule over us. It's not until we, as women, see our liberation through what Jesus Christ came to do will we no longer live our lives playing the role of the damsel in distress.

Man as Savior

As a woman, I know firsthand how some men can be. Just like many women I also struggle with my perception of men. I tend to perceive a man as my Savior as the one that God positioned to protect, provide, and lead me. However, the more I am discovering who Jesus is and what He did, my soul is being liberated and set free from disabling perceptions of men. Now, though I struggle with a fully liberated perception of men it is becoming much easier not to habitually think as the damsel in distress whom I once emulated all the time. Because I no longer perceive a man as being superior to me, I no longer think of myself as inferior to a man. Instead, I am learning to think about myself through the mind and thoughts of Jesus Christ. However, I notice that some men who live under the superior thought process of the curse of Eve will not come anywhere near a woman who does not present herself as being inferior to men. The curse of Eve causes many men to purposely seek out women to whom they feel superior. Consequently, men bound by the curse of Eve look for docile women who will allow them to rule and control the home with no say from the woman at all. Due to their fallen nature, many men look for damsels in distress whom they can rescue and to whom they can show their salvation. Unfortunately, when a man perceives himself as inferior to a woman whom he deems as being confident and stronger than he is, he digresses into feelings of emasculation. Sadly, once an abusive man perceives himself as being weaker than a woman, he can become jealous and do everything in his physical and psychological power to downsize her so that he can feel like the strong one. Any time a man constantly feels like his wife is his enemy, or vice versa, that marriage is headed for disaster. How can two people become one if a person perceives his or her other half as the enemy? Truthfully, any time a couple is motivated by jealousy, competition, and the desire to control and rule the other, that relationship does not reflect God's original order in any way, shape, or form. When we look at what God established in the beginning, we can clearly see that when it comes to marriage, whatever prestige, power, self-esteem, confidence, etc., the wife has, the husband also has, and vice versa. God is and will always reflect the essence of "one" in a marriage.

Dead Man Walking

Life is too short, and I believe that the way a man lives can add years to—or subtract years from—his life. Of course, this fact applies to women as well. However, according to the Centers for Disease Control and Prevention, men suffer in higher numbers from:

- Suicide—3.53 times more often than women.
- 24.3% of men suffer from heart disease as compared to 22.3% of women.
- Men live 76.1 years, while women live 5 years longer (81.1 years).

I sometimes wonder whether the reason men live shorter lives is that they are trained to carry the weight of a "god"—a weight that mortal men were not created to carry. Men were never created to do everything alone, to be the only ones who have all the answers, the only ones that set the rules, the only ones who dictate plans, etc. Nope, not at all. God sets the standards that both male and female follow together, helping one another. God expects a man to learn how to follow God, not to be a god. God expects a man to join to his wife, become "one" with his wife, and walk with her equally as a team, helping one another accomplish the same goal of building a healthy family and being prosperous under the supreme rule of God. Maybe when many men see that following Jesus

Christ requires them to change the way they regard women and to understand that their current behavior is not adding any years to their lives; instead, it is adding pain, depression, heart problems, suicide, false responsibility, habitual unfaithfulness, and a string of broken relationships. Maybe once men in the Christian church who are blinded by the curse of Eve recognize that something is terribly wrong with their beliefs and perception of women, they will discover that they are missing Jesus in their hearts.

The Unloved

Sadly, due to the perception that stems from the curse of Eve, while many Christian men seem to be taught to love, value, and sacrifice themselves for women, they never seem to be taught to love and value themselves. Sometimes I wonder whether some men feel as though they are simply workhorses, used for their ability to make money and provide. Perhaps they feel that this is as far as their value goes. I believe that any man who thinks this way is left in a constant state of feeling unloved and undervalued by women. Sometimes I wonder whether that is the reason why many men seek sexual pleasure more than an emotional connection with a woman. I sometimes feel as though many men gain their sense of self- worth from their sexual performance and the size of their wallet. I wonder whether all the responsibility to love and carry the weight of taking care of another person causes men to use unfaithful behavior as a means of escaping from the pressure they feel. Because many women within the Christian church are taught to respect a man and not love a man, I wonder whether some men feel as though a woman wants them only for what they can provide and not for who they are. In my opinion, how can a husband truly love and connect with his wife faithfully if he has been convinced that God does not deem him deserving of love from his wife? Anyone who thinks that God requires only one person in a relationship to love the other and only one person in a relationship to respect the other is preventing the formation of the "one" connection. Sometimes, I wonder whether some Christian men feel as though loving the woman is entirely their responsibility, and all the woman has to do is sit, be fit, and look good for her man while he carries the full responsibility for the home. I believe that when a man thinks under the curse of Eve, he feels as though he is obligated by God to take full responsibility. In a bitter response to what he has been taught is "God's order," he sometimes can behave heartlessly toward a woman.

Two Wrongs Don't Make a Right

Today, because so many women—both inside and outside the Christian church—are so fed up with the habitual bad behavior of many men, these women have turned the tables in their relationships. Sadly, today, many women cheat on men more than they ever have. Many women have good jobs and strong careers and are even becoming abusive toward men. Some women even aim to be the superior ones in the relationship and they use their money and prestige to control men. Some women do all these things to get back at men who have been behaving this way for years. Now, some men are literally crying serious tears because they don't like the treatment that women have been dealing with for centuries, both inside and outside the Christian church. Sadly, the fellas are also rebelling. Many men are tired of feeling like women are using them for their money, so they are closing their wallets and creating new tactics for dating so that they are not taken advantage of. Unfortunately, some men are also turning the tables on women and seeking women with money so they can take advantage of them. I could go on and on about the very divisive behaviors in which both sexes are engaging, inside and outside the Christian Church. It seems like the relationships between males and females are becoming more intense, all while the Christian church keeps preaching and teaching the same doctrines that have absolutely nothing to do with the unity of God, which can be seen only through the liberation sent through Jesus Christ. Jesus represents life, equality, love, respect, and unity between the sexes, and it is a shame to watch so many sweet, innocent, yet beguiled members of the Christian church fall all over themselves while confessing the name of Jesus and putting on full display the thought processes that are derived from the roots of the curse of Eve.

It is never okay for a man to mistreat a woman, and I don't like watching a woman mistreat a man. A woman should never habitually demean, dominate, or seek to control a man, and vice versa. As my mama used to say, "Two wrongs don't make a right." When it comes to relationships with the opposite sex, if a man wants a woman to respect him, he must practice respecting her. The same applies to the woman's attempts to gain respect from the man. Instead of men and women battling one another over who is stronger, smarter, or greater, both males and females should practice genuine communication and understanding of one another. I realize that all males and females were given emotions to express and the same amount of love and respect to share. However, if we never seek God by following Christ's instructions, we will never see our equality to the opposite sex. Sadly, if people continue believing the misperceived doctrines preached within a large majority of the Christian church today, the sexes will remain trapped under the curse and living at odds with one another.

Long-Term Pain

I know some women who have been married much longer than I was—some for 15, 20, 30, or 40 years to a man who did nothing but suffocate the remnants of their souls. As a matter of fact, most of the time, throughout the entire marriage, the relationship was a nightmarish event with one- sided submission to pure emotional torture that was extremely painful for the woman. A large majority of the Christian church will back the husband, to the detriment of the woman's soul and, sometimes, endangering the safety and well-being of the kids, with no apology or remorse. The majority of the Christian church does this because they think that they are doing God a service by following what they perceive to be God's order. However, in reality, the church is upholding the standards of what one person wrote as being superior to the freedom that Jesus died to restore to both males and females. The majority of the Christian church completely ignores the initial plan that God orchestrated and has chosen to follow a pattern extracted from the perception of the curse of Eve and reflected in the former Old Covenant laws.

I have noticed that when it comes to marriage, according to statistics, women file for divorce much more often than men do. Yet, it seems like so many men have no idea why women seek divorces. Many men don't understand that both men and women were created for a relationship with one another. These men have to understand that their money alone will never be good enough to keep a woman satisfied. In reality, although finances are important, all women want is to be treated with respect, like human beings. They don't want to be treated like slaves, sex objects, or second-class citizens. A women should never feel like she is being paid by the man, just to stay quiet so he can get away with whatever he wants. In reality, today, many women make their own income, with or without a man. So overall a woman will value human decency and respect from a man more than any amount of money a man could ever pay.

Why Do Women Do What We Do?

Although it is frustrating to see so many men who are blinded by the curse of Eve, I am also upset and very hurt with women. I am upset with myself for doubting God's love for me and for assuming that I was doing Him a favor by staying in an abusive domestic relationship for two years. Although two years is not as long as the period of time that many women endure, or have endured, in abusive relationships, it is still two years of my life that I will never get back. It seems that we women waste so much time with men who are blinded by the curse of Eve. We don't realize that these blind men will never change if they don't see the need to change by allowing

God to expose their selfish, unloving hearts to them. Sadly, we think that we are supposed to embrace and accept these crazy behaviors as the norm.

Why do we refuse to believe in Christ? Is it not evident that the curse of Eve still has us, as women, longing for the love and affection of men who do not love themselves or us? Why do we, as women, fill up more church buildings hearing about Jesus, yet allow ourselves to stay in abusive relationships as if that is what Jesus is asking us to do? The woman's suffrage movement of 1920 paved the way for many of the rights that women enjoy today. Also, not only have laws that once allowed men to rule over women been biblically destroyed by Christ, but male-dominated laws are being naturally overturned and confronted all over the world. The "Me Too" and "Church Too" movements have shown us women that we do have a voice and that our voices are effective. Over 2,000 years ago, Jesus liberated women once and for all. Knowing all these facts, why do we, as women, still allow men to continue using us for sex, banning us from serving God in leadership positions within the public forum of the Christian church, destroying our dignity, tearing down our self-esteem, and disrespecting and abusing us? Then, on top of all that, they leave us emotionally tattered and torn, by ourselves, raising children whom they helped to create. Sadly, this behavior is expected outside the Christian Church because men outside do not claim to know Christ; therefore, their lives depict the curse of Eve as the norm. Yet the same bad behavior perceived from the curse of Eve outside the Christian church is seen at extreme levels among many men within the Christian church. The truth is, Jesus took abuse so that we don't have to. It is an insult to the very nature of the love of God to continue allowing ourselves to be subjected to outright mistreatment in the name of God.

Now, my heart goes out to women who feel stuck in relationships because of fear of harm or lack of economic strength. However, as our awareness of the fact that God values and loves us grows along with our self-love, we should realize that national hotlines and state, county, and city agencies have been established to help victims of domestic abuse transition out of volatile situations. After going through my situation, I founded an organization called Empowering Christians to Overcome Abuse (ECTOA), which offers informative resources and spiritual support to women who are going through abusive situations. Currently, the organization is small, with an informative website to give guidance.

The truth is, I am disappointed overall with male and female behaviors toward one another. Men don't deserve to be disrespected and used for their money, while women don't deserve to be disrespected and used for their bodies. In general, aside from the misperceptions within the Christian church, males and females are first and foremost human beings whom God created equally, with a plan and purpose. We were literally created to love and respect one another and yet we are choosing to live far below our purpose, in hate and disrespect for God and one another.

The Stigma of Divorce

I believe each curse represents a different negative outcome. The curse of Adam represents a broken relationship with God and the curse of Eve represents a broken relationship between men and women, which, in turn, affects the family. It disrupts a heart-to-heart connection between all humanity. Therefore, I believe that divorce is the outcome of the fall of Eve. Within the Christian church, respectfully, due to God's heart for unity, divorce is not encouraged. It is looked down upon and can be harshly judged as if it were an unpardonable sin. Because of the Biblical stigma, many Christian women stay in abusive marriages rather than get divorced. In my case, when I got my divorce, I was fully aware that God hates divorce along with several other things. I was also fully aware of what Jesus said about divorce in Mark 10:1-9:

"Then He arose from there and came to the region of Judea by the other side of the Jordan. And multitudes gathered to Him again, and as He

was accustomed, He taught them again. The Pharisees came and asked Him, 'Is it lawful for a man to divorce his wife?' testing Him. And He answered and said to them, 'What did Moses command you?' They said, 'Moses permitted a man to write a certificate of divorce, and to dismiss her.' And Jesus answered and said to them, 'Because of the hardness of your heart he wrote you this precept. But from the beginning of the creation, God 'made them male and female.' 'For this reason a man shall leave his father and mother and be joined to his wife, and the two shall become one flesh'; so then they are no longer two, but one flesh. Therefore, what God has joined together, let not man separate.'"

Well, you can imagine how I felt after reading these verses. I mean, even my husband used these verses to scare me and keep me in the marriage. Truthfully, his fear tactics worked for a very short while until I sought God for guidance in all this. Considering how much I love God and want to please Him, if I thought that my desire to leave did not please Him, I probably would have stayed in the marriage and lost my sanity and peace in my soul because of it. However, I found myself asking the question: Is this really a marriage? Is this really love? Thankfully, the Lord began to unveil His heart, showing me that, although my husband and I had a piece of paper, our hearts and minds were already separated because of outright dishonesty and abuse on his part. Because God looks at the heart to define who is or is not married, He let me know that the environment for my marriage was not one that His Spirit will ever honor. The Lord let me know that my husband's behavior toward me was not rooted in His love at all. He let me know that His character of love had nothing to do with abusive behavior. God's definition of marriage is very different from a mortal man's definition of marriage. God pointed out Mark 10:9 and showed me that if my husband and I had really been married according to His standards, connected by His heart and perception, habitual abuse would not be present. Instead, our relationship would have been a breeding ground for the seven pillars I mentioned earlier: communication, honesty, humility, love, respect, transparency, and trust. Well, of course, after hearing my Father's words with tears in my eyes, a broken heart, and a cracked soul, I courageously left my husband and divorced him a short while later.

However, even after the Holy Spirit gave me peace about Christ perception of marriage and divorce, I still believed that my ex-husband could change and that we could reconcile. Because I still had hope that our marriage could survive, my divorce felt like a death that I despised and desperately hated. However, another point that helped me get through the pain of my situation was understanding that God experiences the pain of a divorce. People walk with God and then leave His path in their souls and hearts all the time. Does He like it? No, not at all, but He knows it is going to happen. In 2 Peter 2:9, it says:

> *"The Lord is not slow to fulfill his promise as some count slowness, but is patient toward you, not wishing that any should perish, but that all should reach repentance."*

Now, that verse clearly says that God wishes that we would all repent, but the truth is, God knows He created humanity with the free will to make a choice. God knows that not every living human being will choose to repent and approach Him through Christ. Once we, as His followers, understand how the curse works in our lives and relationships, we will see that when Adam and Eve disobeyed God's instructions to not eat of the forbidden fruit, humanity immediately fell out of a relationship with God. Once that happened, a divorce took place from the beginning. This is why God hates divorce. Divorces show the evident fruit of discord and a life lived outside God's order of unity. In my case, I knew that Jesus had taken abuse on the cross so that I did not have to. I knew that abusive behavior was outside the legal boundaries of the order of God's love, established before the curse of Eve. The abusive behavior under the curse had already separated me and my husband. My liberated mindset and perception of Christ restored my mind back before the curse. However, my ex-husband's habitual abusive behavior under the curse prevented us from ever joining together as one to fulfill what God had ordained. The Greek word for "joined" in Mark 10:9 (the underlined verse) is "synezeuxen." That word is defined as *"to fasten to one yoke, yoke together, to join together, unite, of the marriage tie."* Once we understand what it means to be joined together for the essence of "one" to work, the man and the woman must think, value, and perceive God's original order above their own desires. They must open their hearts to one another and receive one another with mutual submission, love, and respect. To be truly joined as one requires both individuals to truly open their hearts to *"fasten themselves together"* in their hearts and souls. However, in many marriages, the only thing holding the relationship together is a piece of paper. To people, that paper reflects the status of their relationship as married, but really, in their hearts and minds, they sometimes don't really know one another—or even like or love one another. For instance, if you don't believe me when I say that God is more interested in the hearts of those married than He is in the paper, think about how many people misuse marriage to get what they want. Some people will legally marry to gain access to the citizenship of another country. Some people marry for sex, for money, or as a cover to pursue unnatural desires. Sadly, even pedophiles will use marriage to prey on the innocent kids of a single mother. Today, same-sex marriages are legal on paper, and soon marriages with animals and other unnatural relationships will become legal as well. However, what do you think God would be more concerned with: people simply obtaining the piece of paper, or people obeying His standards and boundaries of love? and being married both in their hearts and on paper? For the record, I do believe in upholding the standards of a legal marriage that God has created between one man and one woman. I do not believe that God will honor or bless any relationship He deems unnatural. I believe in legal marriage, and it is in our best interests to obey the laws of the land. However, when it comes to the heart that God is truly looking at, the paper holds more weight legally in the hands of mortal men than it does to God. God is a heart reformer, not a paper pusher. He will not encourage a person to focus solely on running after a piece of paper, without first checking the temperature in their own heart. What bothers me is that if God says sin (bad behavior and actions outside of God's boundaries) separates us from Him, what makes us think that He will make someone stay in a marriage in which habitual sinful behavior causes separation? The Bible says that God will blot names out of His book of life. This basically means that He will remove the names of those who were once married to Him in their hearts (Revelation 17:8). Basically, God will remove from His Heavenly roster the names of all those who are habitually unrepentant. Yet, according to the majority of the doctrines within the Christian church, a Christian who is supposed to follow God is bound to stay in a marriage with a person who habitually behaves in a way that devalues another person to the point that even that person's habitual unrepentant behavior causes God to grab an eraser. Nope, I don't think so. I find it amazing that so many people within the Christian church think they can habitually misrepresent God with no threat of a lost relationship with God or anyone else.

Most Christians are taught that marriage is a covenant held between a man and a woman. Most Christians are also taught that a covenant between two mortal human beings is held on the same level as God's relationship with humanity, as if neither marital relationship can be broken. However, the Bible is clear that a person can break a covenant with God. A person can break a fastened, yoked-together marital relationship by making a habitual choice to disregard the standards of God's love sent through Jesus Christ, which keeps each relationship together. For this reason, the "once-saved- always-saved" mantra that is a popular belief in the Christian church does not fly with God. So, if a person can break a covenant with God, why is it so hard to fathom that a joined marriage between two people can be broken as well? Sometimes, that which has been broken can be resolved, and other times, it cannot be resolved. It all depends on the person's heart yielding to humility and truly seeking sincere reconciliation with God and the other person.

God is the one who creates the structure of all relationships, and humanity is supposed to follow His model. If you don't believe me, just look at the Ten Commandments. Basically, what separates us from God will always separate us from one another (Exodus 20). Truth be told, the mindset of the abused will constantly be in conflict with the mindset of the abuser because the victim does not like being abused— and rightly so. On the other hand, the abuser really does not like it when the abused refuses the abuse. Understandably, both the abuser's and the abused's perceptions of love will clash. The perception of the curse and the liberated perception we see through Christ will always be at odds. Our mindset under the curse will always destroy our relationship with God and our relationships with each other. Unfortunately, due to the two different perceptions of God (one veiled under the curse and the other liberated through Christ), my divorce was impossible to avoid. I wanted to include and share my revelation about divorce because, within a large majority of the Christian church, the fear of being punished by God and judged by others for getting a divorce is, sadly, causing many women to risk their lives by staying in abusive relationships. Hopefully, this information will help women overcome the stigma of divorce.

The Essence of Time

Now, please don't get me wrong. I believe that everything in life is about timing, and time spent in an abusive relationship should be considered based on each individual case. However, I believe that if physical abuse is taking place, an automatic termination is in order. On the other hand, when it comes to verbal and emotional abuse, each person must know their limits and also be aware that sometimes these two forms of abuse have been known to transition into physical abuse. In my case, I prayed and sought God for guidance. The Holy Spirit prompted me to reach out to a domestic abuse organization that educated me about domestic abuse and helped me safely transition out of my relationship. I suggest that because every domestic abuse case is different, each person should draw strength from God, be led by the Holy Spirit, and reach out for help from a trusted source (e.g., domestic abuse support organizations, friends, or family). In some cases, the man who is abusive may be going through a rough time and may need prayer, space, outside counsel, and time to help himself get through his abusive behavior. However, if the man is determined to continue in the relationship without seeking or accepting help, if he gaslights you and is a narcissist who blames you for being the cause of his bad behavior, if he makes excuses for his behavior and refuses to uphold the seven pillars that I previously mentioned, the marriage is an illusion and not really a marriage—to God anyway. God created marriage to involve two people who are willing to equally carry the weight of the relationship and to do whatever is needed to build a healthy relationship between the two parties. When one person refuses to participate and cooperate with their other half, that marriage becomes off- balance and usually ends up crumbling under all the weight. Sadly, the woman in the marriage is usually the one who is left standing alone; she usually suffers from deep-seated emotional wounds. She also feels spiritually displaced and discouraged because, sometimes, she feels like she let God down. These standards also apply to men who are in abusive relationships. Sadly, men sometimes end up emotionally broken and left alone to stand for their marriages as well.

CHAPTER 13

UNDERSTANDING LIBERATION

Growing up, I learned only about the curse of Adam. The curse of Eve was never taught or even mentioned in the Bible except in Genesis. However, the Bible refers to the curse of Adam several times. Based on the verses we discussed in previous chapters, it is clear that the curse of Eve has been alive and well and in full effect in the Christian church for centuries. Because of what the Bible says about women, I never knew my full liberty as a woman—a liberty that came through the death and resurrection of Jesus Christ. As a matter of fact, I was never taught the fullness of what Jesus did. All I remember being told is that no one could ever know the fullness of exactly what Jesus Christ did. It seemed that because no one could ever really know His fullness, the essence of

God's character and heart was overlooked and literally lost by a few writers or translators of the Bible.

One thing that really helped me understand Jesus Christ and the Old and New Covenants was understanding God's character and heart. Several Christians within the church sit like I once did, with little to no understanding of the fullness of what Jesus did. Many people don't know the difference between the covenants. All I was raised to know was that Jesus loved me, that He came, died, and rose again so that I could go to church, give my time and money to God through the church to maintain my blessings, and not sin. I know now that since Christ has come, there have been a lot of misunderstandings about what Jesus actually did to separate the Old Covenant Jews from the New Covenant Christians. Once God revealed the meaning of Matthew 5:17-18 to me, the revelation of these verses helped transform my thoughts, reestablish my beliefs, and liberate my perception to see Jesus. In Mathew 5:17-18, Jesus said, *"Do not think that I came to destroy the Law or the Prophets. I did not come to destroy, but to fulfill. For assuredly, I say to you, till heaven and earth pass away, one jot or one tittle will by no means pass from the law till all is fulfilled."* At one point, these verses were very confusing to me. I would say, based on what I have learned in the Christian church, this passage of scripture is probably one of the most confusing passages in the Bible. Although we know that God is not the author of confusion, this does not mean that people understand everything that the Bible says. I know I have no idea about the meaning of some scriptures, but the verses that the Holy Spirit reveals to me always seem to break every trail of confusion in my life. So, in an effort to share what I believe the Holy Spirit has graciously revealed to me I will break down these verses piece by piece. However, before I explain what I believe to be the correct, liberating perception of these verses, let me explain other perceptions first.

I have found that there are three ways to perceive these verses. First, these verses allude to the fact that Jesus did not destroy any part of the Mosaic laws. He somehow fulfilled the purpose of all 613 laws. Due to this interpretation today, some people who call themselves "New Covenant Christians" dismiss repentance. They live lawless lives with no repentance to God or apology for anyone else, behaving as if Jesus died for all their sins once and for all. They embrace His grace without having any desire to repent and change their sinful lifestyles. Basically, those who believe this way are embracing the "once-saved-always-saved" belief. Those who believe this way do not feel accountable to God or anyone else.

Another perception of these verses today is to believe that when Jesus came, He opened the gates to the Gentile Christians, engrafting them into following the Mosaic laws with the Jews. This perception is what I was raised to believe, and it is what most Christians believe today. Many Christians believe that their blessings come from following the same laws as the Jews, while simultaneously receiving their salvation through Jesus Christ. I have found that, when it comes to understanding the Old and New Covenants, this is the most popular and widely believed perception from most Christians. So, in essence, most Christians perceive that the covenants are the same, with vast similarities and few differences. Some of the vast similarities are as follows: The Jews have their holy Sabbath (Friday sunset to Saturday sunset) while the Christians have their holy Sabbath (Sunday); the Jews have rabbis in synagogues (soon the priest will reenter the rebuilt temple and resume formal ceremonial laws) while the Christians have Pastors in churches; and the Christians pay tithes and offerings to churches while the Jews give according to the Talmud. (Many Jews in the synagogues do not use the terminology "tithe and offerings" because, currently, there is no priest in a temple to receive them.) Traditionally, according to the Jewish history found in the Mosaic laws, men were superior to women, and women were subjugated by men. (Today, relationships between men and women within the Jewish community are more reflective of the equality shared in Genesis 1:27-28, which is part of the Jewish Torah—the first five books of the Bible.) Today, although the number of women in leadership is increasing, traditionally women have been banned from leadership within the public forum of the Christian church, just like women were and are still banned from leadership in the historical Orthodox synagogues. Based on Biblical history, when the Jewish temple is rebuilt in Israel, women should not be allowed to serve as priests. So, here we see that, yes, there are several similarities between the Jews and the Christians. As I mentioned in Chapter 1, the only real difference is that Christians verbally accept Jesus as the Messiah prophesied to the Jews in the Old Testament, while the Jews neither received nor accepted Jesus Christ as the prophesied Messiah. So, now the Jews are waiting for their Messiah, who to the Christians will be the Anti-Christ.

In a nutshell, now we know the predominant similarities and differences between the Jews and the Christians. Learning these similarities and differences helped me on my road toward being liberated in Christ.

Now that I have explained two out of three perceptions, let me explain the third and final one. After I had that amazing encounter with God that I shared in the Introduction, God opened the eyes of my heart to see His heart behind His words that He sent through Christ. Once I saw these verses through Christ perception, they liberated me. I was able to understand what Jesus' death and resurrection did to bring a final separation between Judaism and Christianity, which ultimately liberated me as a woman.

First, for me to fully explain what these verses mean, if you don't mind, I must repeat the information from Chapter 1 about the details of the Mosaic laws. As we know, the Mosaic laws are split into three parts: ceremonial laws (consisting of God's process for redemption, which was given through the Jewish high priest selected by God to present blood offerings on behalf of the Jewish people in their temple), moral laws (the Ten Commandments), and civil laws (laws that instruct the order for relationships between men and women: Women are to be submissive to men as their superior, the ways in which men and women should and should not dress, nutritional diets, how to treat the dead, punishment by either stoning or death for breaking the law, the outlawing of tattoos, allowable and forbidden sexual relations, etc.). Once I understood the three parts of the Mosaic laws, I was able to understand how to interpret those verses. When Jesus died, He became the final sacrifice replacing the need for the blood sacrifices offered by the Jewish priest in the temple. The word "fulfill" in verse 17 literally means to "deliver, complete, fill up…" while the word "fulfill" in verse 18 means "to become, to come into existence, to begin to be, to receive being, to be born, to arise, come on, appear, of occurrences in nature of life…" Therefore, I learned that the one part of the Mosaic laws that Jesus fulfilled and replaced the need for was the ceremonial laws. Based on the second definition of the word "fulfill" in verse 18, I learned that once Jesus died, out of His blood poured the loving standards for the New Covenant perception of God. Once Jesus became our redemption, the civil laws that detailed the physical punishments for breaking the laws (stoning and death) were removed as well and were replaced with the grace and mercy that are seen and perceived only through belief in Jesus Christ. The true path to seeing Jesus is paved with repentance that brings forth change in a person's soul, heart, and beliefs. This, in turn is seen as visible evidence in a person's life. Once we understand that, the next question is: What happened to the rest of the civil and moral laws? Basically, verse 18 is saying that no part of the Mosaic laws was allowed to be touched or changed until Jesus Christ died, became the final sacrifice, and allowed His life to take the place of that entire system. Once Jesus died, He redefined the focus of God's heart, reestablished the foundation and perception of the Mosaic laws, and redefined what was relevant and important to God. Jesus basically upgraded the Mosaic laws. His death broke the mental thought process of Adam and Eve. In doing so, Jesus destroyed the perception that humanity must do good things to be good and gain salvation, attention, and acceptance from God. He also broke the perception that sets the male sex as superior to the female. Under the second perception, the tediousness of the exterior parts of the Mosaic laws (no tattoos, what a person wears or does not wear, what a person eats or does not eat, keeping the Sabbath, tithing, temple duties, the temple structure, approaching one man in the position of priest as mediator between God and humanity, men being in a superior place over women, etc.) is followed with more of a concern for how God judges the individual exterior deeds of a person rather than with a concern for what God focuses on the most. So, what is God concerned with the most? To God, the sincerity of heart that is found in the essence of a relationship between Him and humanity, men and women, and all general relationships, is more valuable than any individual deed within itself. This is the reason why God is not as concerned about whether or not a Christian pays tithes or offerings to a church, gets a tattoo, recites repetitious prayers, goes to Mass, gets confirmed by the church, has a pastor, eats pork, wears pants (applicable to women), goes to church on the Sabbath, etc. All these tedious deeds become pointless to God and irrelevant to the value of the inner motives of the heart. Truthfully, if a person has love in their heart, lives in a constant mindset of repentance (change), and truly has a relationship with God sent through Jesus Christ, yet that person does not consider these monotonous details, that person will not go to hell. However, if a person does not have the love of God and does not live a lifestyle of repentance (change) sent through Jesus Christ in his or her heart, and focuses only on following every tedious religious detail, that person will be dismissed from God's presence on Judgment Day. God prefers true heart-to-heart fellowship between Him and one another to the stale attendance of a weekly service with no heart for God or the people with whom one is in attendance. The heart of a person cannot be changed by simply going to church, doing good deeds, paying tithes, wearing (or not wearing) certain clothes, being connected to or having the covering of a pastor in a church building, etc. A person's heart can be transformed only when they meditate on thoughts that are rooted in God's character and reflective of His loving heart, expressed through the death and resurrection of Jesus Christ. Then, once a person receives and acknowledges what Christ did, His standards of love should be meditated on. When that happens, a person can develop beliefs that become an anchor holding the character of God in one's heart. Once those beliefs are buried in a person's heart, that person acts and behaves differently. That person's attitude reflects God's character, which is rooted in the person's heart. Now that person's eyes are able to view life through Christ perception. This is how the head of Christ becomes attached to each individual member of His body. Once a person perceives God through Christ, the foundation of their good deeds is no longer based on performing good works as a bridge to approaching God in an effort to gain His attention and maintain His blessings. Instead, because of what Christ has done, one does good deeds with sincere love and concern for the person receiving them.

As a woman, when I saw the fullness of what Jesus did by breaking the curses of not just Adam but of Eve as well, I was liberated. I was able to connect to God through the revelation of the fullness of what Jesus Christ has done through His death and resurrection. Thankfully, as a woman, when I saw that Christ represents liberated love, His love was the strength I needed to overcome my abusive situation and transition my mind from the deadly poison portrayed by the overall concept of the Christian church.

The Rise of Liberation

What exactly does it mean to say that Jesus "broke the curse"? When Jesus Christ died, He did so on a mountain named "Golgotha," which literally means "the place of the skull." So, when Christ died, He destroyed the pattern of thoughts that trapped humanity into thought processes, beliefs, and perceptions that left men and women separated from God and one another. If Christ had never broken the superior thought process in men and the inferior thought process in women, then men and women could never have been joined together to build fruitful families based on the essence of one. God desires sincere, heartfelt relationships with His creation, through Jesus. He desires to see the family unit grow, and to experience compassion, love, respect, equality, empathy, and justice within all of Humanity. So, for God to accomplish the vision of family and unity within humanity, He needed the curse of Adam to be broken. That way, people can be restored back to Him. In addition, He needed the curse of Eve to be broken so that relationships between men and women could be restored and the family structure could be rebuilt according to His original order.

If the Mosaic laws alone had worked, the train of thought that comes from the curses of Adam and Eve would have been broken. However, as we know, that was not the case. This is why it is crucial to believe in Jesus and what He did. His train of thought encompasses the character and heart of God, which teaches individuals to value and love themselves, connects men and women to God, and unites the sexes to one another (according to God's preordained sexual boundaries). God loves people more than he cares about tattoos, what a person wears or does not wear, what a person eats or does not eat, who keeps the Sabbath, who pays their tithes, etc. Now, don't get me wrong. Is maintaining a good diet going to help us all live longer? Absolutely. Is dressing modestly and respectful a good idea? Yes…absolutely. However, if a person dresses distasteful and eats terribly all their life, they are not going to hell for that. (Even if they know Jesus, they may see Him much sooner if they don't maintain a healthy diet.) Truthfully, a person will not go to hell for disregarding the Sabbath day by not attending Sunday morning services in an isolated church building. Also, because our bodies are the temple of the Holy Spirit, we follow God through our belief in Jesus Christ daily from our hearts (Luke 9:23). Once the standards of a liberated relationship with God are embraced, the Sabbath is lived in peace and rest in our hearts every day. I could go on and on detailing the tedious laws; however, there is no need. Overall, these tedious laws, do not reflect our relationships with God and one another, and unless a relationship is effected to God those details are not important.

As I mentioned previously, the Ten Commandments are what keep relationships together, and the sexual relationship standards (God ordains and accepts male and female relationships, God forbids and rejects bestiality, incest, same-sex relationships, sexual relationships with children, adultery, etc.) come from the civil laws. When the relationship standards in the civil laws are maintained through God's standards of love sent through Jesus Christ, these laws, in essence, keep the human population healthy and growing. Once we understand what is important to God, we understand why a change of focus was needed. At one point, following the Mosaic laws did not require love for God or others; it was all about the duties and the blessings that came from following God's laws. Before Christ, every Mosaic law was carried out under the perception of the curse of Adam; everything was about following those laws to gain God's acceptance and blessings. If the people did not follow those laws to the "T," they were in for harsh punishments or death. Because the Mosaic laws complemented men under the curse of Eve, men always seemed to hold the superior position over women and to maintain a dominant role in the Jewish temple. Traditionally, if women did not comply with what men said, they were disowned, looked upon as disobedient, and immediately replaced. Meanwhile, the bad behavior of men got a clear pass from the Mosaic Laws.

I don't believe God ever liked this; however, because humanity rejected Him, He could not interfere again without the final blood sacrifice of Jesus Christ. When Jesus came, He shook those laws of old, switching the foundation of all relationships from obeying God in an effort to gain God's attention and blessings to obeying God as one who has God's attention and blessings through Christ. Now we are to perceive God through what Jesus Christ has done for us by obeying His commandments; we can love ourselves and have a loving relationship with God and true unity between men and women. In essence, we show our love for God by showing His love to one another through word and deed.

Once I understood that, as a woman, I am just as important to God as a man is, and that God created both men and women on equal terms with different attributes that complement one another, that understanding helped liberate my thought process so that I could see God much more clearly. I now see the value in cultivating a healthy relationship with a man and maintaining healthy relationships with family and friends. I no longer live in a constant state of condemnation and shame, stoning myself for everything I do wrong. Now I am honest with God and myself. I repent, think differently, and try to learn from whatever mistakes I make. I now know that just because I stumble into sin, I don't have to stay there and settle into that fallen state. I am also aware that I don't have to live in a long, drawn-out state of condemnation, feeling as though I must pay God through the portal of the Christian church for everything bad that I have done. Instead, I know that God loves and cherishes me, and that His longing desire is for me to have a heart that loves and cherishes Him, myself, and those around me. I realize that life is way too short to throw stones and condemn myself, or anyone else, for what another person has done, or is doing, wrong. I can now boldly speak the truth with a heart full of God's love. If the loving truth of God's word offends people, I cannot control another person's perception of the truth. All I know is, once I saw Jesus, my understanding of God and His plan was liberated. I was able to see God and understand the beauty and value of my self-worth as a woman, as well as the value and self-worth of a man.

Now I realize that God has called me to live my life daily through Christ's liberation, free of the perceptions of Adam and Eve that once imprisoned and veiled my mind with no hope of change. Now I get to gather with no walls of restraint in my everyday life, putting the loving order of Christ's commandments on full display. Based on the understanding that God has revealed to me about Jesus Christ, I no longer feel the weight of obligations to follow all the tedious laws that have made it mandatory for me to go to church, pay my tithes to church leaders, sow my financial seeds into prominent ministries, wear what people deem to be holy attire (long dresses, no makeup, clergy robes, etc.), do good deeds to provoke God's blessings, etc. Nope, I realize now that my body is a temple for God's Holy Spirit to dwell in. Now I make a conscious decision to think with the mind of Christ and to allow His head to be mine. I try to allow God's Holy Spirit to lead me in my daily life, to make a liberated choice to fellowship when, where, and how God leads me. Because Christ has liberated me, I genuinely love people and desire to see people fulfill whatever God has called them to do. At one time in my life, I gave solely to prominent Christian ministries out of obligation and a desperate need to see God bless me and secure my life and livelihood. Thankfully, because I am now liberated, I don't give of my time and money for the sole reason that my blessings and financial security depend on it. Instead, I joyfully share whatever I can with whomever I wish, simply because I love others and choose to help from a heart of pure concern. I do all I do now because Jesus Christ has blessed me with liberated love. If that means investing in a friend's business, I will do that. If it means simply helping a friend or neighbor fix a vehicle, buy food, etc., I will do that. If it means giving of my time and money to a non-profit organization to fund and support a cause I believe in, I will do that. If it means choosing to attend a formal Sunday morning service when and if the Holy Spirit leads me to do so, I will do that. For me, liberation has brought my mind into a constant state of euphoria. No matter what happens to me, I know that the God of the universe loves me so much,

He sacrificed His only Son for me—for little ole' me to live liberated in His boundaries of love. I now know that if I am ever confined to a bed without a means of taking care of myself and reach the point that I am unable to give a dime to anyone else ever again, God will know my heart and still love me and provide for me, simply because He genuinely loves and cares about me. As a woman, the liberated love of God sent through Christ is rebuilding my self-esteem and self -Value.

I know I am not perfect and thank God for that, Because perfection is not what God ever asked for. Thankfully, all God wants is sincere repentance, true humility and honesty from my heart, and for me to at least aim to love Him, myself, and others. When I fail, I know that His loving mercy will always forgive me and pick me up. God wants me, as a woman, to hold my head up high and know that I am just as smart and knowledgeable as a man is. I know now I no longer have to feel as though God favors a man over me. I know now that the relationship laws are written on my heart, and when I hurt God, myself, or someone else, the Holy Spirit reveals those laws and convicts me to change so that I can fulfill my purpose to love all people, regardless of how they live.

Although I may not agree with every lifestyle choice a person makes, that does not mean I have to shun a person or look down on them. I realize now that I don't have to treat a person differently because that person does not have a pastor, go to church, or pay their tithes. If God does not care about all those tedious and blind religious details, neither do I. God cares about and sincerely loves people, and now so do I. I can love everyone equally because that is what I was created to do.

With all that said, once the majority of the Christian church realizes that how they think about God, corrupts their beliefs and imprisons their perception toward God and male and female relationships, they will do as I did and as I still do: Repent for being more concerned about tedious laws and then start following the commandments to love according to the example that Jesus Christ left. Once the Christian church is truly liberated in Christ and starts teaching God's unified standards for male and female relationships, the quiet domestic abuse within the Christian church (which has also affected those outside the church) will come to an end.

CHAPTER 14

CONFESSIONS OF A LIBERATED WOMAN

After leaving my husband and learning that the beliefs I had been taught by the majority of the Christian church had contributed to my collision with domestic abuse and had stripped me, as a woman, of the God-given dominion and liberation I had received through Jesus Christ, I realized that I had to do a few things: I had to take a deep breath, look in the mirror, remove my mind from America's version of Christianity, step into the mind of Christ, defuse my own anger, deal with my hurt, and refuse to allow the shortsightedness of many within the Christian church to stop me from living the liberated and peaceful life God created me to live. As a woman, although I am a victim of domestic abuse and oppressive doctrines within the Christian church, I refuse to sit on the pew and remain blind to my God-given identity.

Instead, I am embracing Christ's liberty and allowing His love to give me the strength to continue overcoming the curse of Eve and the mental prison that typically confines victims of domestic abuse. I realize that God loves me and He created me to not only survive but thrive in my love for Him, myself, and others. I know that God has graced me with enough love to share with one special man in my life. As a woman, I refuse to make any man who enters my life suffer because of the blind foolishness from a few men in my past. I believe Jesus Christ is capable of healing all the broken areas of my heart and emotions. I know that God created both men and women with equal dominion to live fruitful lives, fulfilling our purpose to love Him, ourselves, and those around us. I know I can love and respect a man and be loved and respected by a man in return. As a woman, no matter how much pain I have been through or will go through in the future, I refuse to sit in the pew of a Christian church and be taught to live contrary to my God-ordained purpose. I will not allow the cold, dark abyss of bitterness to consume me. I will remain open to a man coming into my life—a man who is being set free from the curse of Eve, just as I am being set free. I am looking for a man who will allow the standards of God sent through Jesus Christ to be the only true foundation of our home. A man who will value the differences in our attributes and understand mutual submission, love, and respect—a man who aims to adhere to the simple, life- changing commandments of Jesus Christ, just as I aim to do the same.

Truthfully, as a woman, why would I sign up to place myself in the bonds of today's version of a "Christian" marriage that is completely opposite of God's original order for marriage? It is so sad how the Christian church paints marriage as being based on one sided submission (on the side of the male), oppressing and encouraging women to live like second class citizens in their own homes, conveying the message that God set mortal men on His level of divinity, and encouraging a dictatorship model for male and female relationships. All while, excusing the disruptive prideful tyrannical attitudes within many Christian men within the public forum of the Christian church. Sadly, what I described is the concept for a Christian marriage and the concept of male superiority is encouraged and promoted by the Christian church. I don't know about you, but I will never again be signing up for their version of marriage. Nope, once is enough for me. My next marriage will be based on God's original version, which requires mutual submission, love, and respect from both the man and the woman in the marriage.

After what I have been through in regard to marriage, I sometimes wonder if I ever want to get married again.

Although I disagree with completely rejecting the legal institution of marriage, I understand why some people frown upon it and refuse the standards for a legal union. However, while I may be unsure about my future in terms of marriage, I still believe that marriage was never created to be perfect; rather, it was created to be a vehicle of intimacy that displays God's perfect love as reflected by two imperfect people. As I always say, it's not the institution of marriage itself that's the problem; it's the people in the marriage who have the issues. In spite of all the foolish behaviors within marriage, I truly see the original bond of marriage, which God created before the fall, as beautiful and reflective of His love on earth. I realize that life is all about choices and that if I decide to get married again, I simply need to make a much better choice than I did last time.

I am blessed to realize that not all men live imprisoned by the curse of Eve. There are some absolutely amazing men out there, and I am happy to have male family members, male friends, and even a few guys I have dated in the past who truly love and respect themselves and women. Men who truly respect women should be celebrated and cherished for their ability to build—not break—a woman. Men who value women and understand how to love and respect them are strong, courageous, and brave for having made the wise decision to simply do what is right to another human being. When a man truly loves God, he will love and respect himself and refuse to treat a woman as his enemy.

Covered in Thorns

Truthfully, the thought patterns that come from the curse of Eve have contaminated my beliefs and stained my perception. As a woman, I see myself and all women like roses blooming into the place that God created for us to take. However, I feel like I live in a world where so many men behave more like thorns sent to stick out of the stems of a woman's life. Those thorny men add pain each time they touch a woman. Sadly, because I was raised with corrupt Christian teachings about men, I will always struggle to not perceive men as more than whom God created them to be. Sadly, as I grow as a woman, I realize that many men (mostly Christian) are the thorns that have caused me pain and done the most to hinder the growth of my life. The narcissistic, sex-driven, and dominant behaviors women have had to endure from many men, both Christian and non-Christian, have actually shown me how strong God created women to be. My heart is really touched and goes out to the good guys out there. The good guys have a fear of God, strong resilience, and the necessary courage to go against the tsunami of contaminated men blinded by the curse of Eve. The good guys who have the mind of Christ are reflectors of God's love and those men will remove the thorns from a woman's life and help her blossom and grow to be the person whom God created her to be.

Truthfully, God's word encourages us to consider the one closest to us to be greater than ourselves. Therefore, if and when I choose to marry again, I will always consider my husband to be my better half. My husband will be the closest one to me, so he will have that honor...and because I will be the closest one to him, he should extend the same honor to me. With all that said, I must be honest and confess that I am still old-fashioned in many ways. I have no problem with a man being a leader or leading me. I love it when a man initiates a relationship and asks me out on a date, opens the door for me, and treats me like a lady. I still like the fairy-tale romance stories in which the strong man comes in, swoops the woman into his arms, and rescues her. However, I do not live my life expecting a man to rescue me, nor do I look to be led or ruled by a man. I absolutely refuse to give the full reins of my liberated life through Jesus Christ to a mortal man who is just as sinful as I am. Nope. Only one man died for me and deserves the full reins of my life, and His name is Jesus. However, I also want to say that, in a sense, trust causes each person in a relationship to be accountable to the other. So, in a way, the trust between each person is like a set of reins that each person holds and that belongs to the other. Although I am open to being cared for and loved (with Christ love) by a man, God gave me the equal right to care for and love a man (with Christ love).

Overall, as a Christian woman, I don't have a problem with men being leaders. Nope. In my opinion, nothing is more attractive than a man who can lead and take charge of a situation. Nothing is worse than a passive man who always waits for the woman to do everything. The main issue I have with the Christian church is the teachings that create counterfeit thoughts that lead to false beliefs and convey the illusory perception that God placed men in a prominent position that allows them to rule over and be superior to women. As we learned, that is not true at all and it is that lie that I reject. To me, men are necessary. They play a vital role in God's kingdom...but so do women. Both men and women were created to love, respect, connect, and walk in mutual submission with one another. God never created men and women to compete, fight, or rule over one another in a relationship.

Destination Liberation

Although I will always love those within the Christian church, I no longer consider myself a Christian if one defines that term according to the popular version, based solely on church attendance, following the complete list of 613 commandments from the Mosiac Laws, being a woman in a one-sided submissive relationship, and doing good works to gain my blessings and prove myself to God. Nope, I don't consider myself a Christian according to those terms at all. However, considering the word Christian is defined as one who follows Christ and no one else I aim to follow Christ. Therefore, I have no problem being called a Christian according to His simple terms of what it means to be a follower of Christ.

Considering, the fact that today's Christian version of a relationship is so far removed from God's original order, I seriously doubt that God perceives me to be the rebellious woman whom I am sure many Christians regard me as, simply because I do not agree with their perception of God, nor do I follow their version of a relationship. Thankfully, I am learning a little more every day about how to live in dominion as a liberated woman and how to walk as a joint heir with Christ as an active member of His body. Now that I have seen Jesus and, as a woman, receiveda taste of His liberation, I have found that the remnants of my brokenness, which the Christian church induced, are ever before me. The more I see my brokenness, the more I realize how human I am and how much I need Christ liberated love to not only survive but thrive in my life.

When it comes to the Christian church, I feel like I am the odd person left out of the Sunday morning cliché. Sometimes it seems as though, as a woman, no matter what I do within the Christian church, my gender will always be considered secondary to the male gender and the man will always be looked upon as superior to the woman. Because Christ is liberating my perception of myself as a woman, I feel like I no longer fit in with the slanted concepts and images of God or of relationships between men and women that the majority of the Christian Church conveys. Unfortunately, I lost my husband to the slanted beliefs within the Christian Church. Instead of my ex-husband reconciling with me and making an effort to fix our broken marriage, right after our separation he bragged about the new Christian church he was attending. Sadly, my ex-husband chose to disregard what Jesus commanded (to love our neighbor closest one to a person as ourselves) and to instead embrace tedious religious details. He joyfully attended Sunday morning services while disregarding God's heart of love and reconciliation. Needless to say, after watching the pews of the Christain church suck the liberated love of Christ out of people I love, I was very upset and hurt, not only with my ex but with the dysfunctional teachings and overall image of the Christian church. I feel like when I divorced my husband, I divorced my Christian pastor too. Unfortunately, because the doctrines within the Christian church are all that I have ever known, and because the Christian environment has been part of my life since I was a child, I am not sure where to go from here. All I know is that my days of blindly sitting on the pew, following corrupt doctrines that have destroyed my value as a woman and stolen the souls of so many I love, are over. I realize now that I must protect my liberation by no longer meditating on teachings that create poisonous beliefs. Truthfully, I am looking to connect with other members of the body of Christ who aim to adhere to Christ's simple loving order. I realize that those who do so are not always found on the pews of the Christian church. I feel like part of me is looking for a new family, one that respects God's original order sent through Christ, more than they respect and acknowledge the order that men blinded by the curse of Eve have conveyed. In reality, my heart and life have been broken by what I have been taught to believe within a vast majority of the Christian church. I am a broken woman who is rediscovering how to live my life unveiled from the curses and outside of the very hurtful and blind teachings within a large majority of the Christian church. Considering the fact that these very slanted teachings are all I have ever known, I feel like I am a child starting over, learning how to think and live in a completely different manner. My heart hurts for so many within the Christian church because I don't think many of my Christian peers are aware of just how much pain this major biblical oversight has inflicted upon women. In my opinion, the most hideous crime of the

Christian church is forgetting who Jesus is and what the characteristics of His loving heart looks like. Once Jesus is seen, the order that God originally created for all marital relationships can be taught, believed, perceived, and followed. It is so sad to see that a majority of the Christian church has become consumed by its own false image of what is necessary to be holy and blessed. At one time in my life, I, along with many of my peers within the Christian church, lived in a way that disregarded the death and resurrection of Jesus Christ. Like most Christians, I was raised to pay more attention to the noise of tedious details (tithes and offerings, who is giving and who isn't, church attendance, who has a pastor, who is wearing the right clothes, etc.), which not even God is concerned about. One important point that many Christians have forgotten is that the mindset that stems from the curse of Adam causes people to focus on the exterior of what appears to be righteous and holy. However, God has always looked, and will always look, at the roots of the intentions of a person's heart. God will always be more concerned about developing a grace-filled heart-to-heart relationship with His people than about His people performing empty, tedious religious deeds with distant hearts and wrong intentions. God created both male and female in His image to reflect His standards of what He declares to be Holiness, Righteousness, and Love. God's main concern is to protect and cultivate the family with His Holy, Righteous, and Loving order. God desires to protect the family unit by ensuring that both male and female take their equal place in sharing the responsibilities of establishing the foundation for the family. Taking care of people within the boundaries of His love is God's top priority. Sadly, the use of God's word to justify the superior placement of men and to demote women as second to men shows just how heartless and far removed from Christ the Christian church has become.

When it comes to Christian men and women, it seems like so many have completely lost sight of the simple love and human respect that Jesus Christ sacrificed His life to express. It saddens my heart to see so many men blinded by the curse of Eve and behaving in such a superior manner. In addition, seeing myself and so many women behave in such an inferior manner by accepting, as the norm, the bad behavior of so many men is disappointing. I am disappointed in myself for having tolerated so much mess at the hands of blind men and for allowing myself to live blind for so long. Yet in my life, the blindness that comes down from the curse of Eve is still very evident to me. Sadly, due to the image of a mortal man as being on the same level as God and due to a mortal man being regarded as the only sex that God uses to create order on the earth and in the home, the broken bonds of trust that many men represent make it seem as though God is the same way. God is known as masculine and is perceived as a man; therefore, because many of us as women have trust issues with men, many of us often times have trust issues with God. Truthfully, what woman would want to serve a God who she perceives deems her to be an inferior, disposable sex object? I don't know any woman who would sincerely serve a God whom she deems as one who dismisses her value. It's so sad to see the image of a very loving and trustworthy God be tainted and distorted by so many of those who portray a false image of His character.

I pray that my Christian peers will see how God is holding Christians responsible for the blood of so many women, all because their spiritual blindness has literally destroyed the very essence of what God intended a relationship to be. While writing this book, I could feel the heart of God so heavy, urging me to let all women know how sorry He is for what we have been through and that He never intended for us to be treated the way we have been treated. Hopefully, those within the Christian church who are still teaching doctrines blinded by the curse of Eve will remember who Jesus is and the fullness of what He came to do. Hopefully, the Christian church will see Jesus and change the direction of their teachings so that they return to the order of God's heart, thereby restoring the foundation of the family that was intended before the fall. Unfortunately, as long as the curse of

Eve continues to blind those within the Christian church, many will continue following His former order for relationships and public gatherings. Truthfully, how can relationships between men and women and the overall community of the public forum of the Christian church be built if those who are supposed to be following God's New order sent through Christ are distracted by the relationship standards and tedious details of God's Old order? Sadly, if those within the Christian church never humble themselves and question what they believe about relationships, they will never confront the falsified perceptions of what God expects from men and women. Consequently, until the true essence of humility enters the hearts of a large majority of men and women within the Christian church, many will never see the mutual submission and dominion that God always intended for both men and women to share. Hopefully, this book will help everyone who reads it change and focus their attention back on what Jesus did so that they can truly see God's original order for relationships. Maybe one day many of those who sit on the pews within the Christian church will see and understand what the essence of being "joined together as one" really means.

Although I have experienced so much pain at the hands of blind men, the liberated love of Christ within me will not allow me to join the ranks of the feminists and hate men. Although, I do understand the plight of a feminist and why many choose to be the way they are, I have no desire to become one. I realize men don't start out as men, but as little boys growing and learning how to be a man and how to treat a woman. Truthfully, the majority of what a man learns comes from what he is taught and that fact is the same for women. Both sexes are victims of one choice made by Adam and Eve Eon's ago. I love and adore the male species and no matter how some men choose to treat women, I have a fear of God and will always aim to respect and love them and any human being regardless of what one believes.

Reality is once a woman becomes liberated, it is very hard to ignore God's original plan for both women and men.

Overall, I pray that men understand that, as liberated women, we are not trying to replace men or move them out of the way. Instead, we, as women, are casting off our inferior perceptions of ourselves and boldly standing up to take our rightful God- given place of equal dominion, next to the man. Hopefully, this book will wake up men and women within the Christian church so that they will take responsibility for their incorrect teachings about male and female relationships. I pray that the Christian church will stop allowing the thought patterns derived from the curse of Eve to blind their eyes from seeing God's original order for male and female relationships. I hope one day they realize the true essence of a relationship with another human being will always require mutual submission, love, and respect. Hopefully, one day many within the Christian church will stop over exalting mortal men, placing more responsibility on men than what God originally intended, and oppressing women all in the name of God.

Well, we have come to the end of my journey. I hope that God can use my negative experiences as a woman within the Christian church as a voice of hope for all abused women, especially abused and oppressed women who are or have been influenced by the misperceived teachings within a large majority of the Christian church.

I hope that by journeying through the lessons and experiences in this book, you now:

- Are empowered to overcome abuse.
- Understand why abusers abuse.
- Know how to perceive God and the opposite sex through the eyes of Jesus Christ.
- Know how to think and believe as a liberated woman.
- Know how to have a simple, loving, and respectful marriage.

I hope that you and I continue to grow and experience the "Liberated Love" of Christ more and more each day. Until our next journey...be blessed!

Scripture References

**All scriptures taken from New King James Version &
King James Version**

Chapter 2
Genesis 1:26-28

Genesis 2:8,15

Genesis 3:8

Chapter 3
Genesis 2:16-17

Genesis 3:1-7

Genesis 3:12-20

Chapter 5
Leviticus 21:7,14

Numbers 5:29-31

Chapter 6
John 8:3-12

Acts 9:3-5

Chapter 7

1 Timothy 2:11-15

1 Corinthians 11:1-16

1 Corinthians 14:34-35

1 Corinthians 3:16

Corinthians 6:19

Revelation 1:6

Acts 1:12-14

Hebrews 4:16

John 13:35

Matthew 22:37-40

Corinthians 12:7

1 Corinthians 3:4-11

Chapter 8

Ephesians 5:1-2

Ephesians 5:19-21

Ephesians 5:31

Ephesians 5:22-25, 33

1 Peter 3:1-7

Colossians 3:18-19

John 5:19

Chapter 9

Corinthians 6:9-10

Timothy 9-10

Romans 1:18-32

Corinthians 3:6

2 Timothy 2:15

2 Timothy 3:16-17

Matthew 15:1-11

Chapter 10

James 4:5-8 Psalms16:18-19 Matthew 5:28

Matthew 15:14

2 Corinthians 10:5

Colossians 3:14-15

Galatians 5:16-18

James 1:14

Chapter 11

Genesis 2:23-25

Genesis 1:26-28

Genesis 2:18

1 Corinthians 13:4-7

John 13:34-35

Matthew 22:37-40

Chapter 12

Matthew 5:17-18

Chapter 13

Luke 9:23

BIBLIOGRAPHY

New King James Version®. Copyright © 1982 by Thomas Nelson. Used by permission. All rights reserved.

King James Version®. Public Domain.

Oxford University Press King James Version with Apocrypha. Copyright © 2008. Used by permission. All rights reserved.

Barnstone, Willis. The Restored New Testament. A New translation with commentary, including the Gnostic Gospels: Thomas, Mary, Judas; Willis Barnstone. W.W. Norton. Copyright © 2009. Used by permission. All rights reserved.

The Holy Bible - The English – Greek Reverse Interlinear New Testament, English Standard Version ® (ESV) Copyright © 2006 by Logos Research Systems, Inc.

Thayer's Greek-English Lexicon of the New Testament by Joseph H. Thayer, Copyright © 2017 by Hendrickson Publishers, Peabody, Massachusetts. Used by permission. All rights reserved.

Porter, Stanley E. The Apostle Paul: His Life, Thought, and Letters, Wm. B. Eerdmans Publishing Co., Copyright © 2016. Used by permission. All rights reserved.

Henry, Matthew. Matthew Henry Whole Bible Commentary.

Public Domain. 1706

Ephesians 5

https://www.biblestudytools.com/commentaries/matthew-henry-complete/ephesians/5.html

Hope Alliance, Round Rock, TX 78664. Abuse Educational Material. Public Education Information. Used by Permission.

Vos, Howard. Nelson's New Illustrated Bible Manners & Customs. Thomas Nelson Publishers. Copyright © 1999 Wilson, A.N. Paul the Mind of the Apostle. W.W. Norton & Company. Copyright © 1997

Mays, L. James, General Editor. Harper Collins Bible Commentary. Harper One. Copyright ©1988 by the Society of Biblical Literature.

The Interpreter's Bible. Abingdon Press Nashville. Copyright © 1955

Ruden, Sarah. Paul Among the People The Apostle Reinterpreted and Reimagined In His Own Time. Pantheon Books. Copyright © 2010 by Sarah Ruden.

Tabor, D. James. Paul and Jesus How the Apostle Transformed Christianity. Simon & Schuster. Copyright © 2012 by James D. Tabor

Gutbrod, Boyd. A Religious Curse – Judeo Christian History. Copyright © 2017 Boyd Gutbrod.

Allberry, Sam. Connected Living in the Light of the Trinity. P&R Publishing, Copyright © 2013.

Legato, Marianne J. *Why Men Die First: How to Lengthen Your Lifespan.* Palgrave Macmillan, 2009.

M.D. Colbert, Don. Deadly Emotions. Copyright © 2003, Thomas Nelson, Inc.

Westfall, T. (2015, Apr 17). Male and female brains. *Journal - Advocate* Retrieved from http://eres.regent.edu

Two Minds: The Cognitive Differences Between Men and Women, Spring 2017, Stanford Medicine Magazine. Article Written by Bruce Goldman.

https://stanmed.stanford.edu/2017spring/how-mens-and-womens-brains-are-different.html

https://www.vocabulary.com/dictionary/abuse

https://ncadv.org/statistics

www.cdc.gov http://www.jewishvirtuallibrary.org/covering-of-the-head

http://www.jewishencyclopedia.com/articles/7432-head-covering-of

https://www.myjewishlearning.com/article/kippah-tallit-and-tefilin-the-clothing-of-jewish-prayer/

http://www.historyworld.net/wrldhis/PlainTextHistories.asp ? historyid=ac66

https://www.biblestudytools.com/bible-study/topical- studies/who-decided-what-went-into-the-bible.html

http://www.aggressivechristianity.net/articles/ecclesia.htm

https://www.biblestudytools.com/lexicons/greek/kjv/hupot ass o.html

https://stanmed.stanford.edu/2017spring/how-mens-and-womens-brains-are-different.html

Westfall, T. (2015, Apr 17). Male and female brains. *Journal - Advocate* Retrieved from http://eres.regent.edu

http://www.apa.org/topics/women-men/index.aspx https://www.webmd.com/men/features/why-mens-lives-are-shorter-than-women#1

https://www.huffingtonpost.com/2013/11/21/us-life-expectancy-oecd_n_4317367.htm1

https://www.bls.gov/opub/mlr/2013/article/marriage-and-divorce-patterns-by-gender-race-and-educational- attainment.htm

https://people.com/crime/teen-victim-confronts-youth-pastor-raped-her-christopher-trent/

https://www.oxygen.com/crime-time/oklahoma-youth-pastor-wilfredo-flores-arrested-for-raping-teen-girl-after-mom-found-him-hiding-in-closet

People Magazine Interview with Bishop Ellis Aretha Franklin's Incident with Ariana Grande

https://www.youtube.com/watch?v=ab5PsQDdEnM

https://www.christianpost.com/news/youth-pastor-arrested-for-rape-after-he-is-caught-in-teenagers-bedroom-226423/

http://dailypost.ng/2015/09/03/pastor-carries-out-oral-sex-with-members-says-his-manhood-is-blessed-with-sacred- semen/

https://www.dailysun.co.za/News/National/pastors-holy-sperm-tricked-me-20160706

https://www.linkedin.com/pulse/pastor-makes-congregants-suck-his-privates-church-has-sanele-justice/

https://thisisafrica.me/lifestyle/pastor-orders-women-strip-kisses-butts-attract-marriage/

http://www.faceofmalawi.com/2014/11/drama-as-pastor-undresses-and-kiss-female-church-members-ass/

http://www.africlandpost.com/nigeria-get-husbands-pastor-undresses-kisses-members-buttocks-beach/

https://www.sowetanlive.co.za/news/2014-11-20-pastor-allegedly-asks-women-to-strip-butt-naked/

https://www.christianpost.com/news/kenyan-pastor-bans-female-congregants-from-wearing-underwear-in-church-115528/

https://nypost.com/2007/05/27/oprahs-painful-years/

https://www.merriam-webster.com/dictionary/abuse

https://www.nytimes.com/2006/04/06/science/06cnd- judas.html

https://www.hebrew4christians.com/Articles/Taryag/taryag.h tml

https://www.blueletterbible.org/nkjv/mat/24/38/p0/t_con
c_95 3038

"Matthew Henry Complete Bible Commentary Online." *Bible Study Tools,*
www.biblestudytools.com/commentaries/matthew-henry-complete/

https://www.chabad.org

https://en.wikipedia.org/wiki/Development_of_the_Christia
n_biblical_canon

https://afsp.org/about-suicide/suicide-statistics/

https://www.cdc.gov/healthequity/lcod/men/2015/all-males/ index.htm

https://www.cdc.gov/women/lcod/2015/all-females/ in-dex.htm#modalIdString_CDCTable_0

https://www.webmd.com/marianne-j-legato

https://www.cnn.com/2017/12/21/health/us-life-expectancy-study/index.html

https://www.catholic.org/saints/saint.php?saint_id=336

https://www.britannica.com/topic/King-James-Version

https://www.britannica.com/topic/biblical-literature

ACKNOWLEDGEMENTS

I would like to thank Yeshua the King of my life, He is my best friend and my most trusted confidant. I am so thankful to Him for revealing His Heart and Liberating Love to me. Thank you, Yeshua, for being my strong tower of wisdom and my refuge for understanding. Thank You Yeshua for allowing me into Your secret place, which daily preserves me and defines who I am. I thank You Lord, for Your grace and Mercy and for giving me the strength to love and forgive myself and those who have hurt me. Even when the pain ran as deep as the sand on the ocean floor, Lord you were always there. Lord, thank You for giving me the strength to overcome! Thank You, Lord, for saving me, raising me, and showing me what it means to believe and live in your Liberating Love! Your love lights up my world! You have made it liberating to admit my wrongs and confess the reality of my shortcomings. Your love has redeemed me from shame and condemnation! I will love and trust You for eternity. With my life, I will say thank You for daily, saving me from living in bondage to my brokenness. I would also like to thank those who faithfully read my books.

I would like to give special thanks, to all my family my mom, my dad Curtis, my step dad Cecil, my brothers Don and Simon, my sister in love Tiffany, my little nephew Jace, Grand mommy, Deb, and every other family member who prayed for me and checked on me while I was going through my situation and my friends Bertha and Michael for being there and opening your home to me and being by side as I cried myself through the remnants of a broken marriage and also to Paul for showing his love and concern as I went through painful moments. Thank you all for your advice, love and understanding. You have all been a huge support as I transitioned from my marriage back to being single again. Your love has been consistent throughout my situation and for that I want to say thank you so much for sharing your liberated love and patience with me.

Passion 4 Purpose Publications would like to thank everyone who participated with the development of Liberated Love…. special thanks goes to…our editors, formatters, and graphics designer for doing such a wonderful job with the chapter heading graphics, and to our awesome back and front cover designers…Shicreta Murray, Russell Smith, Trevarr, Amolbd and to Photographer Edward William Jones for the back cover photo of Shicreta. Special thanks to StarWorx services for always doing a wonderful job on maintaining our P4P website.

ABOUT THE AUTHOR

Shicreta Murray is a prolific Author and Speaker who teaches God's word in a very relevant and clear way. On January 3, 2003, she had an encounter with God that changed her life forever. She heard the loud, thunderous, oceanic voice of God speak to her and tell her to *"Go and tell My people to get their hearts in order because I am coming soon."* Since, Shicreta has received her commission from God, she has authored several books and she teaches people the heart of God through Christ perception. Shicreta lives in Texas where she is the Founder of Empowering Christians to Overcome Abuse (ECTOA).

Made in the USA
Columbia, SC
06 August 2020

15630089R00139